*Management Development
for the Line Manager*

Management Development for the Line Manager

Elton T. Reeves

American Management Association, Inc.

For Ted Edgecomb,
whose needling gave me impetus,
and for my wife, Elsie,
whose love and faith made this possible.

Standard book number: 8144-5179-9

Library of Congress catalog card number:
77-75054

First printing

Foreword

$\mathcal{T}$HIS book is not intended to be a scholarly survey of the field of management development, nor is it a research report on all the studies now being made in the field by the behavioral scientists. It is aimed, rather, at the working manager, to whom management development is only one aspect of an immensely complicated and active work-life. If it helps this manager to clarify his own thinking about the matter, and perhaps points out some shortcuts and some "best ways," it will have justified its existence. Most important of all, it is hoped that a unified and integrated concept of management development as a continuing function will be stimulated in the mind of the reader.

ELTON T. REEVES

Seattle, Washington

Contents

	Introduction	9
1	The Job of the Manager	21
2	Presupervisory Selection	31
3	Presupervisory Training	51
4	The Transition Period—	
	Becoming a Supervisor	73
5	The Middle-Management Desert	102
6	The Second Selection Process	130
7	Executive Development	147
8	Phasing Out an Executive	169
9	Methodology	191
10	Summary	226
	Index	231

Introduction

OF ALL the books and articles currently being written about management development, few if any have presented a philosophic conceptualization of the field as a unified whole. The compartmentalization which has resulted is divisive and shattering. We come to think of presupervisory training as an area in itself, and we fail to integrate it with the necessary discovery of the potential supervisor which precedes it and with the important orientation and introduction to actual supervision which should be contiguous with it.

Moreover, if by some chance we do make this bridge in a logical and helpful way, what then of the long gray years in middle management which have become the great American desert of the management scene? Why do we make a separate entity of the care and feeding of the bright young men who have been tabbed as comers? Executive development will quite naturally tend to be tailored to the personal needs of the individual recipients; but we should never forget that this activity is one planned part of a much larger picture.

This introduction was published in the September 1968 issue of the *Training and Development Journal* under the title "Management Development—A Conceptual Continuum." © 1968 by the American Society for Training and Development.

There is, finally, the inescapable fact that our responsibility to the manager does not end with his arrival at the vice presidential office, but should, in all honor, extend to his preparation for and successful entry into retirement.

Just as the manager's job is cyclical in nature, so the job of management development is a continuing and repetitive activity.

WHAT IS MANAGEMENT DEVELOPMENT?

In its narrowest, most constricted sense, management development is any part of the process by which a manager grows in his job and becomes more promotable. Under this broad definition, chance could be equally as effective as directed activity. It would be fatuous to say that chance does not play a significant part in the development of most managers. As we all know, there are some men who have an amazing proclivity for being in the right place at the right time under the right leadership. We cannot, however, make the assumption that this will happen to every young manager.

As a working definition, this book will use the words "management development" to mean any planned, guided, or directed activity undertaken by a manager to help himself become more competent in his present position or to prepare him for heavier responsibilities to come. Implicit in this concept is a fundamental belief that no man can develop another. In the final analysis, the only one capable of developing any manager is himself. This is in no sense to deprecate the importance of the contribution the boss can make to the process by a sympathetic attitude and planned activities on his part. It simply means that the definitive action is on the part of the individual concerned.

It is becoming increasingly apparent that no modern business can continue to be successful without planned attention to the growth and development of its managerial staff. Two factors are operant here. One is the unbelievably rapid expansion of the technology. To remain even conversant, let alone expert, in the new parts of his chosen field will take a significant chunk of the manager's time in any given year. The second factor is the higher educational level, better training, and increased sophistication of young people as they enter the business scene. This trend will continue. Therefore, tomorrow's manager will be hard put to stay ahead of his subordinates.

THE PLACE OF MANAGEMENT DEVELOPMENT IN THE ORGANIZATION

If the management of any business enterprise accepts the fact that its managerial staff is, individually and collectively, one of the more important assets of the company, it follows without challenge that the process of management development must assume a high place in the hierarchy of business activities. From the working definition assumed here, management development must then intrinsically be a line function. This does not negate the possible usefulness of a small staff of consultant-specialists who have competency in the field. It would then also follow that their reporting relationship should be at the highest of levels, owing to the critical nature of the impact of their work on every level of company management.

It cannot be too rigorously established that, by whatever mechanism this end is accomplished, its importance is of the first order. This has not been easy to sell to the modern American businessman. It is perhaps a little damaging to any man's ego to have to admit that there is room for personal improvement on his part. Similarly, a halo effect may make it hard for him to admit that his subordinates are not miles ahead of their peers. So it is that, to many managers, the whole idea of management development is vaguely threatening.

HISTORICAL DEVELOPMENT OF THE CONCEPT

Management development is nearly as old as recorded history. Moses, in giving his precepts for the leadership of the Hebrew armies, also made provision for the training of replacements for those leaders. The Romans followed a similar pattern, both in the army and in their civil administration. For many centuries, the Chinese picked their governmental leaders on the basis of highly stylized educational requirements. Similarly, the Japanese choose their business managers from the graduating classes of the Japanese universities. Until the most recent of times, British governmental and business executives came from a narrow segment of the population within strict limits of caste and education.

If any one thing can be said to have given American enterprise the vitality which led it to world preeminence, it was the matter of throwing it wide open to the competition of anyone interested. However, it also introduced the element of entrepreneurship. The amazing success in early American history of the one-man business, large and small, probably delayed the emergence of the big American corporation.

Moreover, as some of the first American corporations began to get big, their organizational structures remained fairly flat and the number of managers required was quite small. The period of the 1920's through the 1940's saw a complete restructuring of the American corporation and a great increase in complexity of corporate structure.

It would be difficult to assess the total impact of the American Management Association and the university schools of business administration on American business in the area of management development. Suffice it to say that modern management development is largely a 20th century phenomenon, with its most sophisticated developments occurring since World War II.

FADS AND HOBBY-HORSES AND THEIR EFFECT

Time and again the American businessman has demonstrated our national avidity for the adoption of fads. In a continuing search for the touchstone which will solve all his business problems, he has come up with at least four major fads, all of which have had a considerable impact on the American business scene.

The first of these was "human relations." One of the effects of publicizing the Hawthorne experiments in the 1930's was a tremendous wave of acceptance of the idea that by treating employees as human beings we would solve all our business problems. The logical end point of this idea was that all any young manager needed to be a success was to human-relate. Sweetness and light became the order of the day, and "fire" became a nasty word. If we were threatened with a strike, management's defensive reaction was that we were not sensitive enough in our human relations. But it gradually became apparent that human relations per se was not a golden panacea or the answer to a manager's prayer. The reaction to this discovery was predictably human: If human relations was not the whole answer, then it was no good at all. There came a quick reversal and retreat toward the Theory X position on the part of many managements. This was based on the two strongly polarized managerial positions propounded by the late Professor Douglas McGregor of M.I.T. Under Theory X, he said, management's attitude is that "people are no damn good." They do not like to work, need constant supervision, and will seize every opportunity to sabotage achievement of company objectives. Under Theory Y, the manager says, "They are so good!" Ordinarily, when given good leadership, employees do like to work and will make a worthwhile contribution to company objectives if they are permitted to do so.

The next wave to inundate American business was that of "conference leadership." Now all the manager had to do to be effective in his job was to become expert in leading a business conference. From this expertise there was somehow to fall out, magically, solutions to all his problems. Again it was discovered that this did not necessarily follow. Again there came the reaction, and managers began to look critically at the numbers of conferences held and to wonder if all these trips were necessary.

The third of the hobby-horses still widely current is a fetishism of the word "communication." A manager could seem knowledgeable in the face of a dilemma by looking wise and remarking bravely that the group was faced with a problem in communication. This is often true, but claiming sanctuary in the wilds of general semantics is not, in itself, a solution to the basic problem faced. It is perhaps a hopeful sign that many alert managers are now coming to deny the use of the word "communication" as a sort of adult "King's X" which absolves a man from any responsibility for making a management decision.

The fourth of the fads is very recent and is only now coming into full swing. This is the T-group and its use in training middle management and executives. "T-group," "sensitivity training," and "lab group" are some of the names given to a specialized kind of training developed by the National Training Laboratories. Unstructured groups, under the guidance of a "trainer," live and work together for a period of time, usually two weeks, in an effort to gain greater insight into the individual's personal impact on others. The key to the process is the feedback given spontaneously within the group. We are a long way from a full assessment of the possible usefulness of this elaborate and traumatic training technique. There have been violently positive and violently negative personal reactions to exposure to the T-group. However, it is having a noticeable effect on the management scene.

The thread common to all these fads is apparent. The too-enthusiastic acceptance of any new technique with a total belief in its complete efficacy is inevitably followed by just as complete and thorough rejection of the concept. There usually is a lack of a rational look at what these techniques might contribute to the manager's job if wisely used.

THE PENETRATION OF THE BEHAVIORAL SCIENTIST INTO THE FIELD

There was a time when a young student went on to take his doctoral degree for one of two reasons: He was going to be a research worker or a college teacher. This is no longer the case. Now, industry finds it difficult to recruit all the young men and women it needs who have their terminal degrees. A heavy percentage of the young Ph.D.'s entering American industry today are specialists in the behavioral sciences.

This trend was started by the widespread impact of the Hawthorne studies on the thinking of American businessmen. The possibilities of contributions by behavioral scientists to the business scene are virtually limitless. Personnel research, labor relations, the field of management development itself will give more work to the behavioral scientist than he can possibly get done. The end objective of an industrial psychologist is the prediction and control of human behavior. This is *exactly* the objective of every industrial manager.

It was said that there has been a backlash of reaction following each of the fads adopted by businessmen. This was due to the emotionalism and fuzzy thinking associated with the fads. A large part of the work of the behavioral scientist is in the area of avoiding just such emotional involvement. His entire training is aimed at strengthening his objectivity; every ounce of his persuasive powers must go toward engendering this same objectivity in other managers. The behavioral scientist also learns early in his career that he must not be afraid to make a decision based on the facts at his disposal. Here again, he can be of service to other managers, many of whom still are grossly fearful of making a management decision.

By far the biggest contribution of the behavioral scientist to the area of management development is in his consultative role. He remains as the resource always available to the man who has a managerial problem. If he does not (and the chances are that he will not) have an immediate answer, he at least possesses the tools with which to seek that answer.

The Individual Manager and the Organization

William Whyte has given us the classic study of the relationship of the individual to his business.* All that concerns us here is to remind ourselves that fully half the work of management development is concerned with the manager as an individual. The maintenance of a proper balance between individualism and team membership is the hardest juggling act a manager is called upon to perform. Nothing but his own finely tuned powers of intuition can tell him when he must subordinate self to the team activity or when his best contribution toward achieving the enterprise's objectives will be made by taking a strongly individualistic stand. The middle manager is the one who must repeatedly go through this exercise. He has neither the relatively close supervision of the first-line supervisor nor the much broader latitude of action open at the executive level. This is one of the tests which separate the men from the boys and by which men are chosen for future executive positions.

One critical need in any business enterprise is that every manager be in tune with the overall philosophy of the company for which he works. Innumerable small compromises are a daily necessity with any manager in working for a corporation. If he finds himself in basic conflict with fundamental principles as espoused in the company philosophy, however, his only recourse is to sever the relationship.

---

*William H. Whyte, *The Organization Man*, Simon & Schuster, New York, 1956. The author found the reading of this book a harrowing experience. On five separate occasions he discarded the book, usually with some violence. Each time, however, he was forced to go back and restart it. It is suggested reading for any manager who has the slightest interest in the question of conformity.

LINE AND STAFF RESPONSIBILITIES IN MANAGEMENT DEVELOPMENT

It has already been established as a basic tenet that essentially management development is a line function. This means that every manager who has subordinates reporting to him must recognize his ongoing responsibility for providing the climate in which those subordinates will find it possible to achieve their optimal growth. This climate will vary with the mix of the people involved. Some managers find it possible to be endlessly permissive; others cannot work with subordinates unless they have fairly close controls. This one interlocking and reciprocal relationship between superior and subordinate will strongly color the entire job situation.

The concept of managerial responsibility toward the overall development of subordinates is gaining widespread acceptance. The obverse of the coin is not so widely recognized. Many individuals seem actually surprised when told that they have a fundamental duty to develop themselves to the utmost of their capacities as a regular part of their daily job. This is true even if a manager remains at one level and in the same job for a number of years. With American business now in a continuing state of flux, no job remains static for many weeks at a time.

The staff man's responsibilities in management development are perhaps a little more obvious. He is hired and retained as an expert in the area, and his services to the company will be measured by the degree to which he is accepted as such by line management. Both basic education and experience will contribute about equally to the staff man's effectiveness in management development.

One of the most insidious dangers to effective staff management development work is in allowing the staff man's job to be conceptualized as that of a trainer. His actual training work should be kept to the barest of minimums. His creative and *development* work will be done as a consultant.

Another factor necessary to effective staff work in the field is the ability to relate immediately with employees at every level in the hierarchy. The staff man must be as much at home with a vice president as with a first-line supervisor; his rapport with an hourly worker should be as great as with a department manager.

A Continuing Process—Not a Fractionated Function

Management development is a continuing and continuous function. It is easy to fall victim to tunnel vision as we become engrossed in some of the aspects of the developmental process. It is this absorption in a part of the work that the good manager will avoid. He must be willing to spread his efforts into every facet of management development with about equal vigor.

In this part of his job, the manager is working with the very heart and future success of his company.

I

The Job
of the Manager

*T*HE modern manager has a many-faceted job.
Theoretically, the line part of his activity has not
changed. Actually, as technologies become more complex,
so does the job of the man in charge. Robert Katz [1] recognized this when he assessed the relative importance of
human, technical, and conceptual skills which the manager
needs to do his job. It may seem paradoxical that as technologies become more complex, more *human* skills will
be required from the boss. This is a result of the increasing sophistication and higher educational achievements
of young people as they enter today's business world. The

---

[1] "The Skills of an Effective Administrator," Robert Katz, *Harvard Business Review*, January–February 1955.

superior-subordinate relationship is no longer quite so simple and straightforward as it was a generation ago. Motivation of the subordinate in today's economy is not based on physiological or safety needs; he is operating at the levels of social and ego needs.[2] His job expectations are therefore much greater than were those of his father when *he* started to work. It is part of the job of the manager to provide a climate in which these expectations have a reasonable chance of being realized.

FIVE MAJOR LINE FUNCTIONS

However, as stated earlier, the five line functions of the manager have not changed in basic nature. It is only in their complexity that they make managing more difficult today. Logically, the first of the managerial functions is *planning*. Even before an organization is formed, there must be knowledge of the desired objectives of the organization. Unless we enjoy "shooting blind" we have to have a target in sight before we can function effectively. We should remind ourselves, however, that our present culture does have a terrific impact on any kind of modern business. More than three-quarters of the products now offered for sale to the public were not even in existence 20 years ago. Product life is very short in some industries, making the matter of planning assume even more importance because of the delicate timing involved. All this is not to say that a business firm's long-range objectives

---

[2] Maslow postulates the existence of five levels of need common to every person, the satisfaction of which will act as a motivator. From the more basic to the less, these are physiological, safety, social, ego, and self-actualization. As the needs at one level become fairly well satisfied they cease to act as motivators, and motivational activity goes to higher levels of needs. However, when one of the basic needs is threatened it takes over, and there can be no activity at any higher level until that threat has been removed.

will necessarily change too rapidly, but there may be a quick succession of short-term targets which are mandatory to the firm's continued success.

The state of flux—the general yeastiness—of the American business scene does have a radical effect on any company's organizational structure. The rapid change which we have said is likely to occur in the short-term targets may very possibly require drastic restructuring of the *organization* with much more rapidity than in the past. The aerospace industry gives recognition to this fact of life by organizing itself under the "project" concept. One of the key faculties necessary to the successful manager then becomes almost a matter of intuition. He must become adept at sensing when organizational changes will become necessary. He must also develop a flair for communicating the necessity for these changes to his people so as to create a minimum of resistance on their part. Most people feel threatened by the imminence of change unless its necessity has been clearly documented. It is in this area of interpersonal relationships that a manager will find many of the booby traps in his line activity.

Obviously, the managerial function of *staffing* is also more difficult under the present scene. Unless the manager wants to have a crippling and impossible turnover among his employees, he must exercise consummate care in his personnel selections to insure that his people are capable of great flexibility and can adapt almost instantly to major change. However, if the manager does give this proper attention, it is not so difficult a thing as it might appear at first glance. This is because our young people, as we are getting them in business and industry today, have been subjected to a life of change from their earliest childhood. They are much better conditioned to the kaleidoscopic life than their fathers were. On the other hand, they will also be much more demanding of a believable rationale for any changes proposed. In the final analysis, these more sophisticated young people will demand and get honest communication from their managers.

If the manager has been successful in his organizing and staffing, he will probably find that his function of *directing* his employees will be less onerous than once was true. If the target, the organizational structure, and the personnel involved have been accomplished properly, the people will be capable of much more self-direction than has been the case in the past. Their commitment and involvement will make them more functional within the organization.

The last of the managerial functions in the line—*control*—will take more of the manager's time and attention than it did a few years ago. He is now working with an organism of such delicate complexity that it is imperative that his controls be diagnostic and prognostic rather than reportorial. It will do him absolutely no good to learn after the fact that he has missed a target. Therefore, a significant part of his time will be spent in devising a set of controls which will give him an instantaneous picture of his whereabouts, yet not be so cumbersome and expensive as to be self-defeating.

MANAGERIAL LIAISON
AND COORDINATION

Today's manager is finding that less of his time is being involved in line activities, while more and more of his attention and energy must be focused on his relationships with others in the organization over whom he has no authority. These complex tangential relationships can make or break the manager, because he simply cannot get his job done without the cooperation of this group of peers. (The area of managerial liaison and coordination is in dire need of serious attention on the part of management trainers. For such an important part of the manager's job, there is surprisingly little being written and almost nothing being formally taught in this area.)

A little reflection will show that there are several permutations of different levels of relationships which occur in a manager's liaison work. He has many contacts with his direct peers in the hierarchy—these will probably comprise a majority. But he will also have many meetings, and do much work, with others at both higher and lower levels in the organization. It is here, in the whole area of this coordinating work, that today's manager will find continuously the most rigorous testing of his abilities in interpersonal relationships. Here is also a very pragmatic and selfish reason for the manager's continued maneuvering for the highest possible status he can achieve for his own position. It goes without saying that high status facilitates the work done in liaison and coordination. De facto recognition of this situation is seen daily in the rapidly increasing numbers of seminars being given in this area.

CYCLICAL, REPETITIVE, BUT ALSO CONCURRENT

This "quick and dirty" look at the job of the modern manager should immediately suggest one thing. The various functions which he manipulates are logically cyclical in relationship. Theoretically, there should be a clean, chainlike progression from one management cycle to the next. This, of course, is not the way in which one of our complex industrial organizations actually functions. Instead, the manager will find himself involved in several of his managerial functions concurrently, since he has many different segments of his total enterprise going on at the same time, each probably with a different timing.

THE MANAGERIAL DECISION

Most people accept as a truism that a minister or priest must have what is called a "vocation" before he enters his profession. That is, there must be a conscious feeling of a "calling" which forces him to enter into the field of religion. If management is ever to achieve the status of a true profession, much the same thing must happen in the case of a prospective manager.

There are two ways in which an employee can become a member of management. In the first, he will serve what amounts to an apprenticeship in a succession of jobs of not too much responsibility. Then, either from conscious volition on his part arising from his personal ambition or from being picked by his management as potential managerial timber, he will arrive at the point where he will be forced to make the managerial decision. The second way to enter management is as a managerial trainee. Most such trainees today come from the college recruiting activities of business firms. These young men and women for the most part are the graduates of our schools of business or engineers and scientists, although currently there is an increasing trend toward recruiting "generalists" from the arts and humanities schools.

These two types of managerial recruits have a very different kind of orientation toward the manager's job. The person who has come up through the ranks has in most cases had a measure of contact with unionism in some form. There may even have been inculcated into his thinking strong suspicions of the motives of his company's management. In any event, it is highly improbable that his perspective is broad enough to take in all the factors operant in the thinking of a manager. On the other hand, the young college man, especially if he is the product of one of our schools of business administration, has been strongly influenced toward management's bias.

It is apparent that for long-term success as a manager, any person must make the managerial decision. He *must* align himself on the side of the company from here on out. In many considerations, there must be a complete subordination of self to the good of the organization. Specifically, in many situations there must be subordination of self to the good of the employees working for him. Objectivity of thought and decision must become a cult with him. Just as he has subordinated himself in some things, so must he put his consideration of *any* individual into proper perspective of the group as a whole. He must live as a kind of schizoid for the rest of his life—maintaining a delicate balance between human considerations and those affecting the general welfare of the whole organization.

It will probably be much harder for the man from the ranks to reorient his thinking of a lifetime than it will be for the young college graduate to fit himself into a mold with which his education has made him familiar. However, the person promoted from within has one distinct advantage over his college-recruit rival. Because of his intimate personal knowledge of how he himself used to think in relationship to the company, he will have much more empathy for those he will be supervising than will the young college trainee who will not have had nearly so long an experience as a "worker."

This is not the place to consider the extremely important sociological implications of the managerial decision. Many others have already started to probe the possible effects of the manager's job on his social and domestic lives. Suffice it to say that managership is a jealous mistress.

ATTRIBUTES AND CHARACTERISTICS OF THE MANAGER

The "traitist" theory of managerial leadership persists hardily in the minds of many in spite of overwhelming experimental evidence from the behavioral scientists that it is based on shaky grounds. Repeated attempts to draw up a definitive list of traits necessary in managers have met with failure. Leadership still resists quantification.

In spite of this, it may still be possible to set forth a few traits and characteristics which will facilitate success as a manager.

Motivation. Researchers are in broad agreement that at least three considerations can strongly motivate a manager. Not necessarily in order of magnitude, these are money, power, and status. Obviously, if any or all of these are motivating factors, it will be almost impossible to satisfy them completely and thus reduce or remove their motivational drive.

Objectivity. It has already been stressed that a manager must assume a lifelong mental set in the direction of achieving objectivity, yet at the same time realizing that this will always be a goal not possible of achievement.

Intelligence. It has been shown fairly conclusively that the successful manager will be more intelligent than the average, but not too much more intelligent than those who work for him. The latter situation compounds geometrically problems in communication.

Communication. Probably more managers fail in their entire job from lacks in communicative ability than from any other single factor. And it is perhaps significant that there are many times the failures from undercommunicating than from the opposite.

Sensitivity. In the life of the modern business executive the need for awareness of the perceptions and feelings of those he is working with is increasing every year. He must be sensitive to his impact on others if he is to elicit the cooperation mandatory for the achievement of his objectives.

Tough-mindedness. In direct ratio to his sensitivity, the manager must increase his own tough-mindedness. The road to neuroticism and crackup is paved with his own defensiveness against the attacks of others. His very position makes him an obvious target for others. One of his first lessons must be to roll with the punches thrown at him from every direction.

Integrity. Because of intensive publicity given to those highly placed men who sometimes slip from the straight and narrow, it is easy to drift into a cynical attitude toward the general area of integrity. Honesty, like some of the other "old fashioned" virtues such as loyalty and faith, has come to have almost a comic significance in the thinking of some people. This cannot be too strongly deplored. Every moment of our day-to-day life is built on implicit or explicit faith in the integrity of others. Because of the manager's key position in his business organization, this is one attribute he can never succeed without.

Interrelationships of Functions and Management Development

What has been described thus far (if somewhat sketchily) is a person even more complex than the average human being. His work makes demands on him to which others are not subjected. Because of this inherent complexity, disparities in strengths and weaknesses of the various factors described will be magnified in the manager's job. Well-rounded development and the presentation of a smooth surface in every facet are mandatory to the manager who wants to be successful. In essence, then, his plan for self-development is actually fairly simple. It consists of continuing introspection, self-analysis, and the prescription of remedial activities tending to overcome his weaknesses and take advantage of his strengths.

2

Presupervisory Selection

THE search for new management blood becomes an obsessive, sometimes frantic activity of most managers. Deaths, retirements, and terminations all contribute their part to managerial attrition, but right now our economy is in such a fantastic period of growth that almost every industrial or business concern needs a constant supply of new supervisors with good managerial potential.

WHERE AND HOW DO YOU FIND CANDIDATES FOR MANAGEMENT?

Recognition should be given to the fact that modernization of methods of searching for managerial talent is depressingly slow in many companies. A listing of some of the older methods can only remind us how many of them are still in operation.

Seniority. Many people honestly believe that mere survival in an organization for a number of years is an indication of supervisory potential. Constant union propaganda also has had an effect on the thinking of some. Since many companies are contractually bound to promote their production workers on the basis of seniority, they may succumb to the argument that promotion into supervision should also be on that basis. There is no significant correlation between longevity and the ability to become a good manager. Of course, intimate and detailed knowledge of the organization accrued over long service is an asset to any manager, but only if it is an adjunct to many other attributes in no way connected with length of service.

Nepotism and favoritism. Surviving and rambunctiously healthy in many places is the matter of promotion on the basis of family connections or friendship with present management. It would be hard to argue away the fact that there are many examples of family-held companies which have been very successful through many generations of familial management. But the tide is going the other way. Methods of management which have been successful for many years will not suffice in the future. Decision making is becoming too complex for anyone at the controls of a company to fly by the seat of the pants any more. There are those who will tell us that new supervisors chosen on the basis of personal friendship will have more commitment and display greater loyalty than others. Perhaps. But at best this argument is suspect; we all have friends for whom we would never think of working for any number of perfectly valid reasons.

The best-machinist method. Strongly persistent in some areas is a blind belief that the best workman will make the best supervisor, in spite of the thousands of times we have seen this superstition exploded. Naturally it is important that a first-line supervisor be expert in his area of work. But there are many other factors involved in the choice of a good manager. He will now be getting his work done through other people, rather than with machines or by means of his own hands. Adeptness at work procedures has absolutely no predictive value of success as a supervisor.

Propinquity. Far too many supervisory choices are made in blind panic because of a sudden vacancy in the ranks of management. This, of course, is always an evidence of poor management planning. A backlog of strong supervisory candidates should always be maintained so that two or more choices are available for every opening in first-line supervision. When such provision has not been made, management may point at the nearest man who doesn't have two heads and say, "You are now a supervisor!" Far better to have second-line management cover the vacancy for a time and make certain that a qualified candidate is tapped than to put the wrong person into the job from panicky reaction.

The microtome and microscope methods. Equally to be deplored is the tendency of some to make their choices purely on the basis of exhaustive testing. Intelligence tests, aptitude tests, personality tests, projective tests, attitude tests—you name them and they'll be given. Choice will then be made for promotion on the basis of test results and little else. Just how much can we—as yet—quantify those things that make for managerial success? Unfortunately, not much. Some testing—properly chosen—can of course be a valuable tool in supervisory selection. But it should be *only one* of the criteria involved. A human being operates in too many degrees of freedom for any one independent variable to be definitive in managerial selection.

We have so far been pursuing a frustrating and dissatisfying primrose path leading *away* from good supervisory selection. What, then, *is* good procedure for making such selections? The rest of this chapter will be devoted to examining some of the more promising modern methods of picking those people to whom we propose to entrust a company's future chances of success.

However, before going on, one thing should be established. It is a mistake ever to pick a person as a *first-line* supervisor. He should always be looked at for his potential as a second- or third-line member of management before giving him his first supervisory assignment. Growth potential must figure strongly in the original choice. This is especially significant as we come to realize that the successful first-line supervisor today might not be a success in 10 or 15 years. The job of the supervisor has never been easy; it is more difficult today than ever before; it is not going to get any easier as we go along. In the next two decades, today's successful manager may fail miserably unless he continues to grow into a more complex and difficult job.

COMPANY PHILOSOPHY, POLICIES, AND PROCEDURES

A company's philosophy, whether implicit and discovered only by the employees' intuition and sensitivity or whether preserved in the most formal of written policies, will determine the managerial styles and the image reflected by its management. Any person tabbed for a management position who is not in sympathy with a company's overall philosophy is doomed to failure in his work. It then becomes incumbent on any organization's top managers to assure themselves that most precise communication is maintained down the line in the matter of company philosophy. This becomes especially critical when we realize that first-line supervisors are, in a majority of cases, chosen by second- or third-line management. It is, of course, at the point of implementation—the supervisory area at the first level—that the make-or-break activity occurs to carry out basic management thinking.

It is easy to determine empirically that in far too many cases, little or no real probing is done to determine consonance or dissonance between the thinking of the candidate and the company philosophy. In the particular interactions which occur between management and supervisory candidates, all that is usually required to settle this matter is to ask the man involved. He will be only too glad to communicate his thinking, since he—the one most vitally concerned—will certainly realize the necessity for this harmony.

Policy statement alone, however, is not enough to insure accuracy in matching the candidate to the new job. Because of its broad, all-inclusive, and general nature, philosophy must be implemented with policies and procedures. Definitive value judgments must be made by responsible executives concerning procedures for picking management people.

It is appropriate to point out here one of the dangers inherent in a truly decentralized organization. That is the total blocking which may occur in some departments if the responsible manager fails to agree wholeheartedly with a given piece of company policy. He may blandly ignore it and thereby relegate it to limbo. It could be argued that this is as it should be, since in a decentralized organization the manager has been given total responsibility for his area. Basically, he is accountable only in the broadest of terms to his upper management for the success of his part of the venture. This accountability is usually limited in terms of profit or loss. However, this may mean wide variance in methods of supervisory selection employed in different areas of the same company.

Such total decentralization does not occur in a majority of small and medium-size businesses. Therefore, it can still be said that common sense would dictate a clearly stated and well-controlled series of procedures for picking management candidates. Psychologically, this works as much to the advantage of the candidate as of anyone else. He is a victim of tensions and stresses associated with the penetration of an area totally new and strange to him, and, if he can document his progress through the selection mill by certain easily recognized milestones, it will help to calm his uneasiness and make him better able to show his real potential.

It is not necessary that these procedures be either complicated or involved. In fact, the less they are these, the more functional they are likely to be. The production of large amounts of paperwork along the selection route makes it easy to lose sight of the true objective—the selection and elevation of the very best available candidate for a management position. It cannot be too strongly emphasized that the final selection of a management candidate is the responsibility of the line management involved. The delegation of this function to a staff area, such as the industrial relations department, can only result in big trouble for all concerned. True, personnel specialists may be qualified to give expert advice in the area of aptitudes or attitudes, but they are not in a position to be the best judges of the candidate's overall potential to cope with the particular involvements he will meet in his line. Again, it is often commendable procedure to delegate to staff the function of monitoring for compliance with policy and procedures; this is perfectly acceptable control activity. But no confusion should ever exist about who makes the final choice from among the candidates involved. The responsible line *always* should have the final say.

What has been said here about company philosophy, policies, and procedures has validity in areas other than supervisory selection. But there is no more important aspect of a company's policy activity than in supervisory selection, because each time a new man is elevated to supervision a fairly large bet is being placed on the future security of the whole company. In management circles we hear it said all too often, "After all, he's only a first-line foreman." The word "only" as used here is representative of some very fuzzy thinking. No company is any stronger than its managerial first line. It is the first-line supervisors who make the product.

SUPERVISORY SELECTION COMMITTEES

There is a clearly discernible trend in medium- and large-size companies to make use of supervisory selection committees to administer this important activity. Several advantages can accrue from the use of selection committees. First, continuity of membership will result in a more objective consideration of candidates as committee members get more practice in discharging this duty. Second, representation from each function and each major department will insure that candidates will be given consideration for openings in departments other than their own. Third, the selection of personal favorites will be minimized, since a consensus must be had from a fairly large membership before selection is made. Fourth, a continuing survey of promising candidates maintains general evenness in the search for supervisory potential.

Top management can retain a proper control over maintenance of the supervisory pool by careful monitoring of the committee's activities. Membership in a selection committee, as has already been hinted, is a fine developmental activity in itself. Nowhere is objectivity of judgment held at greater premium than in this sphere of action.

The actual mechanics of administering a selection committee's work are fairly simple. Ordinarily, there must be nomination, personal interviewing, record evaluation, and committee discussion and comparison of candidates prior to the actual selection. The method of nominating candidates presents some special problems which will be considered separately. The process of interviewing the candidates is no small part of the developmental activity for committee members mentioned earlier. Without this sort of interviewing as part of a continuing responsibility, many members of management conceivably could go for years with little occasion to interview strangers formally. Record evaluation of candidate employees on a continuing basis has another bit of fallout of possible importance to the company: The committee membership will exert pressure to see that employee records are kept properly.

Actual committee deliberations will give continuing practice in group decision making of the highest order. The fact that selection is accomplished through group activity in no sense relaxes individual responsibility for the committee members. Rather, it heightens each member's awareness of what he must contribute as an individual to the work of the entire committee.

Selection committees are functional for the organization in another pragmatic way. Their work will be directly geared to the vacancies occurring in the managerial ranks. When movement in management is slow, they can devote this time to more pressing needs.

It is usually true that those companies utilizing selection committees restrict their activity to selection of first-line supervisors and those successive levels reaching into lower-middle management. Ordinarily, executive selection is reserved to top management and the board of directors.

Another facet of the work of selection committees which can benefit the company is the continuing surveillance of general training and developmental needs shown throughout large segments of the employee population. When the committee's activities demonstrate that selection is made difficult because of obvious training lacks, corrective steps can be taken quickly. It is for this reason that staff training and development people should be wired in completely to the moves of the selection committee. Many companies find it functional for a development representative to act as ex officio secretary of the selection committee. The planning of formal training and development programs can be integrated much more smoothly if this kind of liaison is maintained.

One more reaction to the existence of a company supervisory selection committee should not be overlooked. There will be general reinforcement of employee belief in a fair chance for the promotion of all qualified personnel under this system.

It is possible for selection committees to be completely functional under widely varying philosophies. In some companies, these committees have power only to make recommendations for promotion to fill existing vacancies, leaving the final choice to the discretion of line management. In others, the committee makes the final and absolute choice itself, and line management is obliged to go along. Under either of these extremes or

in varying positions between them, the supervisory selection committee can make real contributions to the
strength and stability of a company's management.

VOLUNTEER OR BE DISCOVERED?

There are big differences in protocol between companies in the matter of selection of supervisory candidates.
Some executives feel that one of the criteria by which a
potential manager can be identified is for him to have
enough initiative to announce his own candidacy. At the
opposite extreme are those who feel that self-nomination
is an indication of "pushiness" rather than initiative or
aggressiveness.

There are things to be said for both viewpoints. If
we wait for a supervisory candidate to announce himself,
at least we can assume that he has made the "management decision" and has done some basic thinking about
his own commitment to the company and to management.
This seldom happens without some straightforward communication with at least one other person and perhaps
with several people. If the relationship is at all normal,
he will probably discuss it with his own supervisor. This
communication can act either as a damper or as an ac-
celerator to the selection process. If the supervisor feels
that his subordinate can never make it in supervision,
for whatever combination of reasons, it is his clear duty
to convey this opinion to his subordinate as tactfully as
possible. Of course, this may or may not affect the actions
of the subordinate.

If, on the other hand, the supervisor feels that his
employee has a better than even chance of succeeding as
a manager, he can help in many ways. He can make the
employee's candidacy "official" by bringing his name to

the attention of higher management or to the selection committee. The supervisor can also do many things to facilitate the training and self-development usually necessary before the candidate is fully ready for supervisory appointment.

If a company reserves to management the right to take the first step in the identification of supervisory personnel, strong reinforcement can also be provided for a managerial duty—that of being constantly on the alert for this potential. It is easy for managers to forget for months at a time the importance of this facet of their job. All of us may be prone to tunnel vision owing to the pressures engendered by immediate and urgent goals. The identification of managerial potential in this situation may appear urgent only when actual supervisory or managerial vacancies have occurred. This can then lead to forced choices of what may prove to be unsatisfactory material.

It is generally more customary for a company to compromise between these two extreme positions. Some managerial candidates may be identified and approached by management, while others will bring themselves forward as active candidates.

Whichever of the three methods is used is not nearly so critical as is the conscious adoption and continued use of some formal policy or procedure for maintaining a flow of high-caliber candidates into the area of presupervisory development. This is hard to overemphasize.

In one sense, it might be better for a man to announce his own candidacy. This indicates, as has been said before, his own commitment. In contrast, the man who is approached by management may, under this form of flattery, accept a position for which he has no true and basic aptitudes. (This would make an excellent subject for research to determine the relative success of supervisors chosen by the two methods. It is too important an activity to be left entirely to unsupported value judgments.)

As everyone is aware, pure chance plays a much bigger part in the determination of some people's life work than any of us likes to admit. This is true even in the case of the professions. We all know of a lawyer who took up law after he found it impossible to gain admission to medical school or of some other professional man who had had no personal volitional drive toward his particular life-work activity. This is true in management as well. The number of managers who have "wandered into" management is too large, no matter what the actual percentage may be. As important as competent management is to the economy at large and to our lives as individuals, no manager should ever get his job without rigorous training and proper self-development.

It bears repeating, then, that the actual method of identifying managers is not nearly so important as the activities which become necessary *after* the selection has been made.

THE NUMBERS GAME

The question of how many candidates for supervision any company's management should pick is not always an easy one to answer. There are several determinants which will govern. Is the organization now expanding, or will it in the foreseeable future? What about the general mobility of the management group itself? What percentage of managers is approaching retirement age? How many are being lured away to other companies in a time when management people are in generally short supply?

All these factors have to be weighed and balanced before a definitive number can be attached to the recruitment of new management personnel. For example, one of the better indicators of the state of the economy in general, or in a given industry, is the activity in college recruitment. The lag, however, between picking college recruits and a major change in an industry's economy may be from one to several years. This, in turn, is one measure of the capability of a company's management.

So far as internal choosing of new supervisory potential is concerned, a large percentage of business organizations go by a rule of thumb of "two for one." This means they intend to maintain a reserve of chosen and partially trained personnel about equal to the projected number of actually appointed new managers. So far as planning is concerned, this is unexceptionable. However, there is one latent risk inherent in this procedure which should always be kept in mind by management. That is, no matter how many times a man may be told that no promises are being made because he is being considered for supervision, he will never quite believe this. The special attention he receives at this time is to him an implicit, if not explicit, promise of future action. The normal man does not consider seriously the possibility of his being rejected during the training period. Moreover, the length of time that any candidate will remain satisfied without a promotion is a big variable. More than one company has found itself losing promising employees because they cannot be promoted rapidly enough after they realize they are being considered. Especially if the employee is young and ambitious, without much of his time invested in a company, he may be vulnerable to the blandishments of the competition. This is one of the calculated risks which any management must be willing to assume. Far better to lose a few good people than to find that no one has been prepared at all for a vacancy.

The best procedure for any company to adopt in this

connection is to establish a routine and communicate it as precisely as possible to all employees. Allowance should also be made in planning this activity for a normal bell-curve distribution of response from the candidates chosen. A healthy percentage should be promoted; an equally healthy percentage will, for one reason or another, not be promoted. This is as it should be. Some of the larger companies operate deliberately under a policy of overrecruiting so that they can reasonably expect to wind up with a satisfactory number of qualified managers for their own needs. This, of course, is not possible in smaller and less wealthy operations.

It should be evident from these considerations of the problem that it is going to assume an important and continuing place in overall company planning. It is also fairly obvious that this should be part of the planning of every member of management, since all will be personally affected as well as the organization at large.

The next step in the cycle—how to prepare the candidates for actual entry into supervision—will be looked at in the next chapter.

VALIDITY OF SELECTION CRITERIA

Mention has already been made of several of the older criteria by which men used to be picked for supervision (and, sad to say, sometimes still are). There can be nothing but distrust for seniority, nepotism, propinquity, or pure adeptness at a mechanical job as valid predictors of supervisory success. Yet many closely related factors do seem to be valid as *part* of those things which we look for when we pick candidates for managerial positions. We certainly do attach significance to punctuality and good attendance. We do feel that at least the first-line supervisor should be high in the technical skills associated with the jobs of those he will be supervising. It is a pity that the elements and personal characteristics most closely associated with supervisory success are not as yet subject to much quantification. We all recognize when one man has "good" interpersonal relationships and can persuade other people to his way of thinking. But *how much more* of this particular quality does Joe have than his benchmate Harry? If a dozen peers were to make forced-choice judgments of this quality between the two men, their estimates would probably cover the whole spectrum.

The same, of course, can be said for conceptual skills. Actually, for the most part these skills are latent in any person until put to a direct test. Under the pressure of day-to-day living, it is not common for a workman to do much philosophizing about "the big picture."

Mention has already been made of the danger of depending on a battery of tests as the sole criterion for the hiring of personnel or their promotion within the ranks. This caution might be extended one more step with the proposal that to do *any* testing can be a dangerous thing unless it is administered, scored, and interpreted by qualified personnel. There is a horrifying amount of testing done in our business world by people with absolutely no formal background in psychological testing. A basic core of this sort of test can give valuable insight when properly handled, but it takes an expert to do the job. The so-called dark forest of the personality test is better avoided by any professional personnel people. As has been explained so many times, any "maze-bright" young person can cheat unmercifully in the personality tests so far perpetrated.* The position assumed here is

* E. M. Jennings, *The Executive Autocrat, Bureaucrat, Democrat,* Harper & Row, New York, 1962, shows how this evasion can be accomplished, as does William H. Whyte's *The Organization Man.*

a dangerous one, because it is perfectly possible that by the time this book sees print a personality test may have appeared which is both valid and reliable. When that time comes, what has been said here about personality testing will be retracted willingly.

We should also cock an eyebrow at the fad of using projective tests in the average managerial ranks. It should be remembered that the preponderant usage of these tests is to reveal neuroses and psychoses. Pressured though they may be, the vast majority of people in the managerial ranks would still be classified as "normal" personalities.

Until that day when management becomes a true science, we shall probably have to rely on the artistic side of management rather heavily in a selection of new supervisors. So far as that goes, we should be making a grave mistake in underplaying the value of the judgments made in this area by an "old pro" manager. Even though these judgments may seem because of their swiftness to be almost intuitive, they are amazingly close in a large percentage of supervisory selections. It is in this area that the behavioral scientists will make one of their most significant contributions to American management. A massive assault is currently being made by psychologists on the early identification of management personnel. This is coming to be known as "EIMP" among the psychological fraternity and is being watched closely by personnel people.

An alert management will watch the progress of the behavioral scientist very closely for the next few years with the hope that before too long there will be valid methods and good predictors with which he can choose supervisory candidates with a high degree of success.

STANDARDS OF APPRAISAL

The employee who has been picked for promotion into the managerial ranks must expect that he will "be under the glass" minutely for some time to come. Appraisal of him and his work will not be perfunctory, and it will be going on continuously. This should give him no cause for alarm, so long as he is sure that the standards of his appraisal have been fairly selected and are being objectively administered by those responsible for the activity.

This latter point is where the catch sometimes occurs. One of the facets of formal management development programs during the earlier years of the activity which have led to severe criticism of the whole program was the high degree of subjectivity of some of the elements included in the appraisal methods. It was not uncommon to rate managers on such things as initiative, cooperation, judgment, and even personality. The dangers of such an approach are perfectly self-evident. No matter how hard any man tries, objectivity is bound to suffer when he is working with instruments which place a premium on value judgments. A halo effect or a horns effect will be present no matter how much he may struggle against it. One company used a set of appraisal standards which included these elements. Each member of management was appraised once a year by a committee composed of the boss, the boss's boss, and someone of equal or higher rank from another work-area who was familiar with the subject's work. It was not uncommon for the appraisal meetings to last four, five, or six hours before anything like a consensus could be reached among committee members. How many times can you expect to get complete agreement among any three people about one man's personality? Or about his degree of cooperation? Or, for that matter, about his "knowledge of work"?

Another fallout from this approach is that the boss almost always delays, evades, or completely rebels at interviewing the subordinate on the results of such an appraisal. Whether he is conscious of it or not, being put into the position of having to "play God" is distasteful to any reasonable manager. He is aware of the vulnerability of his position and the strong criticism which may be leveled at him for making such judgments. Then, too, under such a subjective kind of operation, it is possible for a subject to be rated very highly even when everyone knows that he is not performing at anything like such a level. The man just isn't farming as well as he knows how.

Fortunately for all concerned, in the company just mentioned the approach was changed to one of management by results, and everything began to go more smoothly. The different approach made sense to managers, they supported it wholeheartedly, the men being appraised were much happier, and some real gains were made in a short time. No one who has any modicum of intellectual honesty can cavil at the thought of being measured against objectively arrived-at standards which have been previously agreed upon.

Of course, it should be remembered that to some supervisory candidates the whole concept of employee appraisal may be new and disquieting. The fact that they have themselves been appraising others for years is not germane. This has been done on such an informal basis that they are hardly conscious of the process. The boss is O.K., or he's a ring-tailed hairy ape. A fellow-workman is a good man or a lazy slob who never carries his end of the load. Since these sorts of judgments are arrived at almost without conscious thought, it may be quite a shock to face the prospect of being the subject of a formal appraisal procedure, especially when it is indicated that the process will go on indefinitely. This is another area where proper and timely managerial communications are of extreme importance. Properly approached, the candidate will see the necessity for appraisal and even the benefits which may come to him from this activity.

Management has a wide choice of standards to apply in the appraisal of any candidate for supervision. The sine qua non is that they must be objectively arrived at and objectively administered.

IDENTIFICATION OF TRAINING NEEDS

At least three people must be involved in determining what training needs the supervisory candidate has. These are his supervisor, staff training or management development personnel, and the candidate himself. The one least likely to be sophisticated in this area is the candidate. Just as in the medical world self-diagnosis is considered a dangerous thing, so the unsophisticated subject may do himself harm if he relies too strongly on his own appraisal of his training needs. He probably hasn't practiced introspection long enough or deeply enough to be at all sure of his own self-analysis. This is not to say that he mustn't perform such an analysis; but he should be ready, at least at first, to defer to the judgments of his supervisor or staff management development people.

The superior should be well qualified to give opinions here. After all, he does know the candidate's work as well as anyone does. He has subjected him to repeated analyses before tabbing him as a supervisory candidate. If his thinking is straight, he is aware of both the strengths and weaknesses of his man. The management development staff representative should be the one most qualified to put together a package of specifics for training the candidate. His expertise in the area is an accrual of both training and background, as well as much consultation. He also has the advantage of being the unbiased observer, since he is not directly in the line management of the candidate. Working together, the three can greatly expedite the exciting transition process as the candidate makes ready to enter the ranks of management.

3

Presupervisory Training

IT WAS said in the preceding chapter that the decision on necessary training of the supervisory candidate would be made through the cooperation of the subject, his supervisor, and management development staff. It is true that some companies have fairly structured training situations into which they put those who have been designated for supervision. Except for whatever images of regimentation this may evoke in the candidates, it is a viable procedure.

There are some factors which should indicate differences in the training of individuals according to their different levels of education, experience, and general maturity. For example, it is now common for a company annually to recruit young MBA's with the intention of working them into management within a relatively short time. The critical factor here is the rapidity with which they gain the necessary maturity. Although it is usually accepted that these young men will enter management at quite an early age, care must still be taken that they are not "thrown to the wolves" before they have their proper defenses set.

How Much, How Far, and How Deep?

As much as anything else, presupervisory training is best when it concentrates in the area of achieving a mental set necessary before anyone can accept the pressures and responsibilities of a managerial position. This matter should be one of deep concern—and repeated checking —to all those who have any responsibility for the candidate's progress. Once again, it is evident that we are in a highly subjective area and that there are at present no handy-dandy rules or formulas for quantifying anyone's emotional or mental maturity.

There is another trap easily entered by those who supervise management training. In the conceptualization of the body of knowledge necessary for a man to advance in management, we sometimes are guilty of trying to prepare a candidate to occupy a vice presidential suite before he gets the necessary "nuts and bolts" to operate successfully as a first-line supervisor. For example, many companies entitle their formal training for supervisory candidates "premanagement training." Why should this not better be called "pre*supervisory* training"? Admittedly, the nomenclature is hazy here. We many times use interchangeably the terms "supervisor" and "manager." Do we actually mean that the two terms are entirely synonymous? We do not if we look at the practices in the field. We would do better to teach a man arithmetic before throwing him into the calculus.

In this same connection, because of the fairly large numbers of people involved, sometimes a tendency develops to assign classroom instruction in presupervisory training to very junior members of the management training staff. Nothing can be more dangerous, unless they are closely supervised, followed step by step through the curriculum, and checked repeatedly for the attitudes and thinking they are engendering in their pupils. Actually, wherever possible, it is far better to put presupervisory candidates in the hands of the old-pro management training people.

From all this, it would be correct to assume that what is proposed here is different levels of penetration into the varying components of premanagement training. The objective should be as well-rounded an individual as it is possible to achieve at the time of assignment to the first supervisory job.

Another factor becomes important in the assessment of the total training job. That is the question of how long it will be before promotion occurs. Again, time differentials should indicate careful planning. After the candidate has been selected, it is common to give him some immediate training. If a long hiatus occurs between this training and promotion to supervisor, the net result may be negative. Presumably, he has been given a case full of fine, sharp tools which will be useful to him as a manager. Like any other tools, these may become rusty with disuse.

The dichotomy of training objectives is to strengthen weaknesses and to take advantage of present strengths. Once again, then, we should reinforce the necessity for careful analysis of training needs on an individual basis. Much good can be had from carefully designed group training efforts, but they can never satisfy equally the needs of all. Each person involved is going to have some needs different from those of any other person. It is management's responsibility to see that these are satisfied before making the first supervisory appointment.

It is clear, then, that management development activity begins before entry into management. This time should be used actively as a separator of the men from the boys. Far better to find out now that a mistake or two have been made, and to rectify them here, than to have to demote a man who has been unhappy and ineffectual in management for several years. In the long run, the man himself will probably be grateful that he has been prevented from making a mistake which would be injurious to his whole company career.

Some Commonly Used Methods

That part of the management development process which has to do with presupervisory training is given wide attention throughout American industry. The methods of approach are very diverse from company to company. Of the five generic methods used, there are numerous combinations and hybrids to be found. It is true that different companies will have different needs to satisfy, and no one can say arbitrarily that one method should be adopted universally. Neither should it follow automatically that once a business concern has adopted a particular method it should be set in concrete from there on out. An alert management will recognize that changing conditions may call for alterations in its program of presupervisory training. In periods of growth, the sheer pressure of numbers of candidates it is necessary to train may force some compromises both in scope of content and in depth of penetration. It follows that under these circumstances it is going to be more difficult to give each of the trainees the desirable personal attention.

Here, then, are only the main categories of presupervisory training, along with their salient characteristics. There are of course many possible combinations of these general types.

The supervisory trainee concept. Companies which have a formal trainee program usually follow this type of configuration in their training of supervisory candidates. Most often, they recruit a set number of trainees annually from the classes of college graduates in various fields. Some organizations allow for a number of candidates to be recruited internally and given the same kind of training.

Typically, the trainee program will be under the administration of training or management development staff people, who look to line management for advice and control of training content. In most cases, a percentage of the time is spent in formal classroom activity, and this normally is conducted by management development personnel or by specialists in some of the fields covered.

In the larger companies, the trainee program may run anywhere from a year to three years, with 18 months representing a mode of the distribution. It is common to distribute the time among the organization's major functions, with the duration of each segment showing management's appraisal of that function's importance to the enterprise. The objectives of this kind of procedure are (1) to acquaint the trainee with the management personnel in the area and (2) to give him an introduction to the function itself and the way it relates to the organization as a whole. It is quite normal to have the trainee attached to a particular manager while he is in that function—in other words, the trainee reports to that manager for a segment of his training period. He may be given real work projects to do, usually of a staff nature; rarely is the trainee given any sort of line responsibility.

Meantime, a regular portion of his week's work is spent in the classroom, where his studies are divided between theoretical management principles and conferences to clarify the relationship between these fundamentals and the actual function in which the trainee is now operating.

It is routine for each trainee to make regular reports on his training to the administrator of the program, with copies to his functional manager of the moment. Also, each manager to whom the trainee has reported makes out a report on him to the administrator, so that, by the time the trainee has made the rounds, there will be evaluations on him from a significant part of the management of the organization. There are two dangers inherent in the use of such a trainee program. The first is that the trainee will find it unpleasantly reminiscent of the academic atmosphere he has just left and will rebel against it. Many young college graduates get restive before graduation in their desire to come to grips with "the real world." Some of the larger companies regularly include a "packing fraction" in their annual trainee quotas to offset expected attrition from this cause. The second thing that happens too often is that managers will be overeager to detach a promising youngster and pin him to their part of the organization before the trainee has completed the entire activity. This, if allowed to happen often, can vitiate the worth of the whole program. It is only after the trainee has had exposure to the entity that he can begin to get a picture of the entire organization and its objectives.

The success of such an ambitious type of managerial training can be realized only with the strongest kind of support from top managers. They must be willing to implement it with those controls necessary to keep it from being short-circuited. It is common procedure to let the trainee have close control over the function to which his final working assignment will be made. This is under the theory that his personal motivation will be greatest in his area of highest interest.

It can be seen that in the main only medium- and large-size companies can hope to implement this kind of program in all its ramifications.

The temporary foreman. The second method of pre-supervisory training is, as the name indicates, the use of supervisory candidates in the actual job of the foreman for short periods of time. The man who has been selected as a possibility for supervision occupies a first-line supervisory job for vacation relief, sick-leave coverage, or any other necessary absence of the regular foreman.

As in so many other cases, there are arguments for and against this type of training activity. On the plus side, the candidate is put squarely into a real-world situation, with all the necessary decision making which goes along with it. He knows, of course, that he has immediate access to the second-line supervisor; but, if he is serious in his desire to advance, he will hesitate to go there for advice unless he really feels that his problem is unusual. Management also has a unique opportunity to see the candidate react under fire much sooner than in the more formal or academic approaches to presupervisory training. The third advantage to the temporary-foreman method is that both the man and the managers will get some sort of feedback from the workers as to how they feel about the candidate's operation. Psychologically, this method is in consonance with the theory of incremental (spaced) learning. If the candidate gets this experience spaced over reasonable intervals, there is every reason to suppose that his learning of the foreman's job will be on a solid basis.

On the negative side, it may be argued that his experience in one sense of the word is not real at all. Everyone—managers, the man himself, and the workers—knows that the situation is artificial by reason of its short duration. A candidate will have a tendency to avoid making any decisions of a policy nature for the area. Neither is he likely to listen to suggestions the implementation of which would require any basic changes in working methods. Even in a grievance situation he is in a special and threatening position. He knows that if the grievance should go through more than the first step or so, he will not be in the position of a supervisor when called upon to help in the final settling of the grievance. Many workers have different attitudes toward a temporary foreman and toward a regular supervisor. There may be just that shade of disrespect which will precipitate a direct confrontation which the regular foreman would not be faced with. Union representatives may have, or may feel that they have, much greater leverage with a temporary foreman than with the regular one.

These negative factors may combine to put the candidate into a particularly trying situation. No matter how badly he may want to be promoted into the supervisory ranks, he knows that during a temporary upgrade nobody around him thinks of his situation as actually being changed. In the minds of his peers, he is much like the school pupil who was chosen by his teachers to be a "monitor." No matter how he may squirm to avoid it, his fellow workers will consider him a traitor to his class. His union relationships become strained and may suffer irreparable damage. When he comes back to his own work group from his temporary upgrade, he will probably undergo a period of ostracism of varying duration.

What all this means is that the method of temporary-foreman presupervisory training sets up a situation where there is no clean-cut definition of position and loyalty. The schizoid position of the trainee is in a sense that of a Dr. Jekyll and Mr. Hyde—a difficult one for any person to occupy.

For this very reason, some managements deliberately choose this method under the working theory that the person who can survive the difficulties will be a stronger and more dedicated supervisor. If this is the rationale, management is then under the necessity of providing support for the temporary foreman above and beyond what it would give to the regular foreman. It can never afford to let him appear to be wrong, and above all else it must avoid the appearance of undercutting his temporary authority. If a grievance arises while a temporary foreman is in charge, the company must be prepared to fight it all the way to and through arbitration, even though it knows from the start that it will probably lose. This is the only way that the temporary foreman can find this method of training supportable at all.

So long as these basic principles are observed, many companies have had good experience with the temporary-foreman system. What has been said so far refers only to the situation where the temporary foreman comes from the ranks. It is equally workable in the case of a supervisory trainee, if at that time he happens to be in a function where hourly workers are to be supervised. The trainee may be placed temporarily in charge of an actual line group as his project of the moment, as was discussed in the last section. This, however, is not done too frequently.

The supervisory trainee concept and that of the temporary foreman are, in their pure sense, philosophically quite far apart. In the former case, we are making a graft onto the managerial trunk; in the latter, we are force-feeding a natural member of the original tree. This is not to say that either system is clearly and demonstrably superior to the other. As has been pointed out many times, the situation of the organization and the philosophy under which it is operated will be the determinants of the method chosen.

Classroom methods. Classroom presupervisory training is a compromise adopted by companies which are unwilling or unable to tie up large amounts of money in this kind of developmental activity. Ordinarily, a series of classroom situations is scheduled on a voluntary, off-hour basis. Attendance may be at the request of management, with the knowledge and encouragement of management, or purely at the volition of the trainee himself. Some managers feel that the willingness of the trainee to invest significant amounts of his own time is one of the best indicators of his real wish to align himself with management.

Several approaches may be taken in this kind of class activity, but it is commonest to consider a variety of subjects relating to general management theory, with perhaps a sprinkling of illustrations which attempt to relate these general principles to the everyday job of the foreman. One of the quickest and most predictable reactions from the union will be accusations that management is attempting to undercut it and "brainwash" its membership. The best defense against this is to assure union leaders that such is not the case and to invite them to attend any or all sessions to reassure themselves that management has no machiavellian motives.

One such incident began when notice of a series of off-hour sessions was posted on plant bulletin boards. It was strongly emphasized that no promises were being made for present or future promotions and that any attendance would be purely voluntary. The local union carried bitter complaints to the international union, and the matter was actually under discussion in national negotiations. Company management held firm, the series was held, and it met with considerable success. The secretary of the local union was asked to attend to report back everything that occurred in the meetings. Before the series was over, the secretary was so involved that he became an active candidate for promotion to supervisor.

The leadership of classroom sessions is a continuing problem. So much off-hour activity is involved that it is difficult to get the right sort of managers to involve themselves for such long periods of time. Since they are working directly with personal attitudes and concepts of management, the quality of the leadership is critical.

For some reason, this setting seems to be one in which it is particularly difficult to get the trainees to break down their reserve and begin to interact freely with one another. If the series is designed to run for 20 or 30 weeks, instructors often find that the halfway point has been passed before a true group begins to evolve from the membership. In fact, the group dynamics of this method of presupervisory training are among the most fascinating of any training activity. Suspicions, both of the company and of the other trainees, are likely to persist for a long time. Jealousies, either already extant or engendered in the group, are difficult to resolve. Maneuvering for special position is a common ploy. A startlingly realistic simulation of company politics at its worst can often be seen in these training groups.

On the other hand, this method does give a fine cross section of functional representation, and, as the group starts to evolve, a cross-fertilization of ideas and problems occurs which is hard to duplicate in any other industrial situation. As can be seen, this exercise is likely to be sterile so far as the company is concerned unless the instructor is meticulous in giving feedback to the managers concerned. It is his responsibility to make some very fundamental decisions on individual class memberships and to close the communication loop with management.

One of the prime advantages of this kind of training is that there is no expense involved. Another side effect which cannot be ignored is the continual "pulse taking" that is available to interested management. This random sampling of the organization's population can give valuable insight concerning attitudinal and morale changes.

It is inevitable that a backwash will carry from these meetings into the organization. Friends in the working groups will be curious about what is going on in "the brainwashing sessions." Many discussions are sure to be held in work breaks and lunch periods as a result of these meetings. It is highly probable that the trainees' supervisors will from time to time check their subordinates' reactions to the training.

For the small company or the organization that has very little money to invest in presupervisory training, the classroom method has the advantages already cited. Admittedly, it does not give either the practical experience or the depth of theoretical approach of some of the other methods. Yet it can help significantly in making the necessary decisions for promotion to first-line supervision.

The MAP. The management action plan, or MAP, was developed by a company which had a pressing need for large numbers of new supervisors, was willing to invest real dollars in their training, and had been far-sighted enough to allow itself time to implement this method. After an intensive and time-consuming screening, candidates were chosen on a two-for-one basis. That is, twice as many were chosen as it was projected to promote on a permanent basis. The men were promoted to first-line foreman and were assigned to line management throughout the plant. They became members of two-man teams in their sectors. In other words, each of them became the de facto supervisor in an area, but each worked directly with, and under guidance from, an experienced and highly capable supervisor. So far as operations were concerned, the old timer disappeared from the scene— that is, he remained in the office while the trainee was on the floor as supervisor. Their contacts throughout each shift were as frequent as either the trainee or his mentor thought necessary. Office time together was spent in going minutely over every happening of the day, as well as in intensive study of departmental policy, procedure, and report writing.

One variation in what might be considered routine operation was that, by agreement with the local union, any grievances arising under the trainee would be heard by both him and his instructor-supervisor. However, the decision on the company's position in answer to the grievance was to be purely that of the trainee.

In addition to this quite hectic introduction to supervisory life, the trainees met on Saturdays in the classroom under the direction of various industrial relations representatives for orientation in general company policy, wage and salary administration, and contract interpretation as well as in interrelationships with other functions such as engineering, accounting, industrial engineering, purchasing, maintenance, and quality control. At the end of the third month the trainees began to get exposure to higher echelons of company management, and at the six-months' banquet they all met and talked with the company vice president of manufacturing.

At the end of one year, as a result of exhaustive evaluations made by many members of management, exactly one-half of the trainees were assigned to regular positions as first-line supervisors and the other half were given the choice of repeating the year's internship or returning to their former jobs. In a very small percentage of the cases, the trainees were not given this choice, but were returned to their regular line. Most of the trainees who were passed over at the end of the first year elected to take a second round of the training.

Regrettably, no scientific evaluation of this ambitious program was ever made. It is probably significant that the large plant in which the MAP program was instituted did succeed in filling its increased supervisory requirements by means of this method. The purely subjective evaluation of the program by top plant management was highly complimentary and remained so for several years thereafter. Again, it is regrettable that no specific follow-up was made of the subjects to determine their relative mobility after this kind of training. In effectively doubling first-line supervision in many areas, the company obviously invested hard dollars in no inconsiderable amount. This was done in the belief that, if they had close control over the training and promotion of a large number of new supervisors, the final outcome would be both economical and generally salutary. The only alternative would have been to recruit significant numbers of supervisors from the outside, and this the company was unwilling to do. It believed strongly in, and practiced, a policy of promotion from within, and it also felt that the costs of recruiting outside supervisors would have approximated the costs entailed in the training program.

This rather lengthy description of an almost unique kind of presupervisory training has been given because it is believed to be an illustration of truly enlightened management. A defense of the proposal, because of the hard dollars required, had to be taken to the board of directors. This was done in the belief that the proposed training would be in accord with overall company policy and would also satisfy the need for additional supervision by the most viable method.

The seminar approach. Anyone who differentiates between the classroom method and the seminar approach might be accused of splitting hairs. It is true that both operate with groups of trainees varying from 15 to 25 members. It is true that both are under the leadership of an instructor who, in the main, is an authoritarian figure. Here the two begin to be sharply different. Under the seminar approach, much more emphasis is put on demanding participation and involvement of every member of the trainee group. Customarily, a mixture of methods is used, including the Harvard case method, the Pigors incident process, role playing, and some of the simpler types of simulation models.

From this array, it is evident that much heavier demands are put on the virtuosity of the instructor in the seminar approach than in the less-demanding lecture or group discussion situation. It is pressurizing to the student, as well, to have his first introduction to the Harvard case method of learning. This has aptly been called the poor man's decision-making model. The intent of the case method is to simulate, as nearly as possible, the actual conditions under which a manager makes most of his decisions in the real business situation. The case description never gives enough facts to satisfy all the trainees. They always find disturbing the matter of not receiving a "correct" answer when the shooting is finished. It is upsetting, at first, to both the group leader and the students to have the leader abandon his authoritarian position, become *almost* one of the boys, and perhaps have no better answers than any other member of the group.

The Pigors incident process does—at the far end—give a school answer, and in this sense it is more satisfying to a majority of the trainees. For the first few times around, the trainees find little comfort in the fact that a manager cannot turn to a glossary of answers when he is faced with a managerial problem. They feel cheated, and in some cases they actually harbor resentment against the group leader for putting them into this position. After several exposures to either of these methods of learning, the trainee will admit to a growing sense of satisfaction after having thoroughly worked through some of the better cases. Also, the common practice of dividing a class into several small teams of four or five members almost instantly generates a healthily competitive spirit within the group. This is a salient feature of the business game, whether it is of the in-basket variety or one of the more complicated computerized games.

Another advantage of the seminar approach is the self-evident need for assigning "homework" between sessions. For some reason the trainee seems to build less resentment when this is done in connection with a case study or a business game than he does when perhaps less-demanding collateral reading assignments are given in conjunction with the traditional classroom method.

Another good inherent in the seminar approach is a facet of the group dynamics of the trainees. The methods just outlined are naturals for eliciting unobtrusively the best of the leadership qualities of individual members. If the group leader is doing his job adequately, he can find ample documentation throughout a series of training sessions to show which trainees are strong in this attribute that is so necessary to successful managerial performance.

The other methodology listed earlier—role playing— takes greater skill on the part of the leader than any of the others enumerated. For some reason, the vast majority of adult males finds it excruciatingly embarrassing to be *forced* into a play-acting situation. It devolves upon the instructor to be artful enough to create a situation where role playing will seem perfectly natural, allowing the individual trainee to assume a role without attracting attention.

So far no mention has been made of the method by which the trainee will be getting his basic theory as groundwork for the activities that have been described. There are two principal methods by which the trainee can be given the basics. It can be assigned as outside reading, either from selected handouts or from a textbook, or it may be administered in the form of "lecturettes" by the instructor at appropriate times during the class meetings.

Perhaps it would be appropriate at this point to mention the importance of facilities in the whole area of management training. The necessity for facilities that are at least adequate was brought home dramatically in one company within the past two years. Up until 18 months ago, all its management training was accomplished in rooms that, at best, could be described only as poor. Many were inside rooms with no air-conditioning of any sort; chairs and tables were of the most ancient and broken-down types; lighting was insufficient and for the most part from open fluorescent bulbs. Then a magnificent new training facility was completed, with 48 of the most modern classrooms, many with facilities for closed-circuit TV, and two theaters, back to back, with a common projection room. The whole building was air-conditioned and beautifully lighted. The only point in question about the facility was its location—seven to fourteen miles from the various plants. Would supervisors drive the extra distance for voluntary management training? They not only would, but did. Attrition dropped dramatically, and attendance remained at the highest percentage in the company's training history.

THE MANAGEMENT DECISION—HAS THE CANDIDATE AFFIRMED IT?

One result of presupervisory training must be absolute before the training can be considered successful. Both the trainee and his supervisors must be sure that he has affirmed the management decision concomitant with his desire to enter supervision. If the process of introspection triggered by the training is a little painful, so much the better. Any *really* good training should hurt just a little. In the all too subjective "evaluations" given to much of American training today, the principal criterion in most cases has come to be, "Did the trainees enjoy it?" "Was it a fun experience?" This is nonsense. Behavior is rarely changed in a situation that is other than traumatic to the trainee; and, unless there is behavioral change, there can be no justification for the cost of training.

One of the best possible signs that training content in presupervisory courses is valid is to have one or two trainees decide somewhere along the line that this is not for them and quit the course. In one presupervisory class, there was one member who had been promoted to supervision during the progress of the series. At the beginning of one of the sessions, he asked two questions in all sincerity: "Do you really mean all these frightening things you keep saying about the heavier responsibilities and hectic life of the supervisor? Is his job really that insecure?" An hour and 45 minutes later, these questions had been given a good working over. During that time, another of the class members suddenly discovered that he actually didn't want to be a supervisor after all. The definitive point seemed to be when the class was welcomed to the group which is on permanent probation. Even if no other lasting result comes from a presupervisory series, the whole thing will be successful if this point is decided in the mind of every trainee.

The supervisor, too, has a right to this information about his subordinate before going any further with plans to promote him. This basic mental set is the only thing which will make the annoyances, insecurities, and frustrations of the manager's life bearable to him over the long haul. The management decision in essence is not necessarily noble, altruistic, or even professional. It is a calm and reasonable acquiescence to the fact that the good of the company must always outweigh any other personal considerations. Of course, it would be naïve to think that, if the manager feels his own welfare to be seriously threatened, he would do nothing about it. What is meant is that, short of this point, company considerations must receive first value.

Is There a "Best" Method of Presupervisory Training?

The answer to the question whether one method of training is best is already implicit in the previous discussion of the different types of presupervisory training. Each has its specific advantages for a given situation; each has its major or minor drawbacks which make it less than ideal. We are then back to another of the previous theses: that any candidate's presupervisory training should be a hand-tailored affair. Class types of exercise *never* should constitute the whole package of training for any supervisory candidate. Some pragmatic planning involving the subject, his supervisor, and developmental specialists ordinarily can lead to a workable package which will have a fair chance of success in preparing the aspirant for his transition period.

One point has probably not been emphasized enough: the sea of reading in which the conscientious young manager is going to be immersed for the rest of his working life. He has at least a threefold purpose in this reading —avoiding obsolescence in his own field, acquiring a new body of knowledge (management theory), and staying abreast of both fields from here on out. One of the best and most helpful contributions the management development specialist can make to his managers is to suggest to them good, timely management readings. He can perform a service here similar to that which the medical detail man does for his doctors—to condense, to summarize, and to present to the busy doctor what is noteworthy in the medical literature.

In the final analysis, it would seem that the best method of supervisory training must be this tailored package for each individual candidate. There are broad variations in individual methods of learning. Where some people seem to thrive in the classroom or seminar situation, others are lost or totally bored by these methods. Perhaps they find their only real cognitive consonance in the work situation itself. These pragmatists seem to need a job-related atmosphere for any learning to take place. Still others gain great insight from the process of enlargement of their own present jobs, until the activities and responsibility of the next level above them finally become meaningful to them.

Everything that has been said here tacitly reinforces a concept of much heavier responsibility of the manager-supervisor in the area of presupervisory training than has customarily been accepted, or even understood, by the average manager. While it does, for a time, make his own job more demanding, if he follows through with this duty he will most certainly save himself much trouble when he launches the new manager on his career.

Management's Commitment to the Individual (Managerial Ethics)

One thing that has been mentioned tangentially, but has not been put together, is management's commitment to the individual presupervisory candidate. This responsibility is especially heavy if management has itself tabbed the individual for special attention.

First, the presupervisory candidate must *never* be put into a punitive situation. Whatever action he takes in good faith during his time as a candidate must never have a boomerang effect on his future. This sounds much simpler and more straightforward than it sometimes works out in practice. One of the elements high on the checklist of attributes necessary for managership is good judgment. If, during his training, the candidate makes an obviously bad decision, management may overreact. Everyone agrees that any manager is entitled to his share of bloopers; for the same reason, it is indefensible to write off a supervisory candidate for any one act of bad judgment.

Second, management owes the trainee a reasonable time in which to adjust himself to the very different interpersonal relationships which he will find both in his own group and with the new people with whom he is now associating. This is closely bound with the new orientation toward a strange set of objectives to which the trainee is now exposed. It is not to be wondered at if he suffers moments of confusion while trying to make these intellectual and personal adjustments. Management's patience at this time must be especially long suffering.

Third, whenever possible, management owes the candidate experience in real supervisory situations for whatever periods of time can be arranged before his actual promotion. As a corollary to this, the trainee must also have as close supervision as possible without actually hampering his decision-making activity. This means, among other things, that the trainee should be allowed to make his own mistakes.

Fourth, management owes the candidate frequent and in-depth counseling throughout the entire period of his training. Obviously, this duty does not disappear after his promotion, but for his emotional stability it is more urgently necessary during his training.

Fifth, evaluation of the trainee's progress must be continuous, close, and as objective as is humanly possible. Reports to the trainee must be as frequent and candid as time allows. There is no time during his work-life when he is more profoundly interested in "How am I doing?"

Sixth, the training period should be brought to a definitive and well-understood conclusion, resulting either in promotion or in a return to his former situation and an understanding that he is no longer a candidate. In the latter event, it must be made clear that there will be no harmful effects in his later company career.

This chronology of events is not quite so easy or straightforward in its accomplishment as may seem to be indicated here. The whole chain will provide an excellent test of the sensitivity of the managerial group. By putting the candidate in an especially vulnerable position, management has increased its duty to give special consideration to the employee throughout his traineeship.

As has already been indicated, the area of presupervisory training is one in which staff management development personnel are frequently involved. It should be reemphasized that this in no way absolves line management from its involvement and responsibility in the activity. The matter of presupervisory training is too crucial to the company's future for anyone to shirk his duty.

4

The Transition Period—
Becoming a Supervisor

*L*ET us assume that the matter of presupervisory training has had proper attention and examine some other basic changes which the new supervisor will have to make. Adopting for the moment Bob Katz's conception of the technical, human, and conceptual skills which any member of management needs for effective performance, let us look at each of these and see how they will affect a man new in the management situation.

The first of the major adjustments is sometimes the hardest for the supervisor to make. In almost all cases, he has been picked as a supervisor in no small measure because of his superior job knowledge and technical skills. Customarily, he will find it difficult to pass the baton to his workmen and to resist the impulse to step in and do the work himself when faced with a technical problem. In union shops, this is more than a psychological trap; he will be subject to grievances and possible censure from his own supervisor if he continues to do the work himself. On the other hand, technical skills loom so large in the life of the first-line supervisor that it is necessary for him to remain on top of the state of the art. He cannot afford to let himself become obsolete in this part of his job. It is in this area that his crew members will test him many times. They will bring to him technical problems to which they well know the answers in an effort to determine his basic ability as a supervisor. (Their ego involvement in the interpersonal relationships is so great that they seldom will test him in this area deliberately.)

In the pyramidal structure of most American businesses and industrial organizations, the first-line supervisor's need for conceptual skills is not very great. His segment of the enterprise is so narrow that it does not entail great breadth of vision. Moreover, under the close supervision to which the first line of management is usually subjected, he may be actively discouraged from too many forays into "looking at the broad picture." A deviant first-liner can be a big headache to second- and third-line supervision. This fact has in it the seeds of tragedy, because no man should be picked for supervision unless he has given some indication that he possesses conceptual skills. As we shall see, in upper-middle management and in executive slots conceptual skills assume greater and greater importance, and they are the *only* determinant of the top executive's success. He has already passed the necessary tests in interpersonal skills before becoming an executive, and by now he is hiring whatever technical skills he may need.

The new supervisor should be urgently aware that

conceptualization is an area in which he is going to have to do much work if he hopes to be promotable for more than one or two levels. This is his most pressing need for personal development at this stage of his career. Should he meet actual resistance from his own immediate supervision in any attempt to strengthen himself in this attribute, there are still many things he can do on his own to flex this muscle. Now is as good a time as any to start to get a more comprehensive picture of the organization as a whole. Company annual reports should be studied thoroughly. Management communication should be followed, weighed, evaluated, and discussed with other supervisors. Off-hour classwork in economics and sociology will be helpful. A new alertness to the problems of management in other departments should be cultivated, and he should make serious attempts to open new lines of communication with his peers in the other functions. This will have an immediate fallout in helping him on the job, as well as laying the foundation for the larger concepts he will need later.

In almost any department there are, from time to time, special-assignment activities which will broaden the knowledge of those who assume them. Volunteering to take on a reasonable number of these will be helpful in developing conceptual skills. Of course, reason must be used so that this extracurricular activity does not impinge too severely on his regular job. Judicious use of the management development staff specialist can also be helpful.

Implicit in this activity is the understanding that the new supervisor's concept of his own new job is progressing and growing in a healthy manner. He will receive inputs from his people, his supervisor, and his peers which must be sorted, evaluated, and put into proper perspective before he can find his own most viable method of operation. He will be judged not only by the results he obtains, but also by the directness and economy by which he achieves his part of the organizational goals. The quicker he can build a workable concept of his job, the quicker he will be an efficient operator.

CHANGES IN INTERPERSONAL RELATIONSHIPS

A plexus of changes will be undergone in the new supervisor's interpersonal relationships. Five groups of relationships are of major importance: with his new subordinates, with his own supervision, with a new peer group, with his family, and with his informal social groups.

If he has been transferred into a group as a new supervisor, he will have to establish a complete set of relationships with his subordinates. In one way, this is the easier situation, since his work group will tend to regard him as *the* new boss, rather than as *a* new boss. There will be the usual probes for soft spots in his armor and the customary jockeying for position by his people. Every individual will have to make his own basic decisions as to how he can best handle interpersonal relationships with subordinates. This will center essentially around how well he knows himself and secondarily around his knowledge of his people. Some supervisors like to have frequent social contacts with their subordinates; others follow a policy of no fraternization; many others fall into positions between these extremes.

The other situation, and in some ways the more difficult, is the one in which the new supervisor has been promoted from within the group. This may be the source of much disquietude to the supervisor. No matter how much he resolves that "there will be no difference" in his relationships with old fellow workmen, this is beyond his control. There *will* be changes. Old friends can overnight become enemies, either because of their basic distrust of managerial representatives or because they are jealous of his promotion. The very process of asserting his new leadership will in itself apply a great deal of stress to old relationships. The new supervisor will have at best only a few weeks or months in which to adjust to this change. He must make many individual re-evaluations, whereas each of his subordinates must make only one. A prominent warning sign should be displayed to the new supervisor here. Overreacting to this changed circumstance can be dangerous to his long-term relationships with his people.

The new relationship with his own supervisor will not entail so great a change as will the relationship with his subordinates, but it will be more subtle. First of all, the new supervisor may be ready to accept his role as a full-fledged member of management while he is still on probation in the thinking of his own line management. He is a pledge in the fraternity, but does not himself recognize this situation. For one thing, he will find that his interactions with his supervision are suddenly on a more formal basis. While he was an hourly worker or in the general office category, he may have been on a highly informal, first-name basis with many members of supervision within his group. Now, for many reasons, this will be changed. His supervisor must avoid any appearance of favoritism or special privilege. Casual social contacts previously enjoyed will suddenly be curtailed, if his boss is one who subscribes to the no-fraternization school of thought.

If the organization maintains a highly professional posture among its management people, the new supervisor will find himself baffled by the observance of protocol now demanded of him. He will be much more severely bound by the necessity of going through channels than he has been used to. Some bosses are hypersensitive to even the appearance of a subordinate's going around them in the chain of command. To balance this there will be the recognition by others in management of his newness in the position, with usually a sincere desire to help him become oriented in his new world.

Some new supervisors are confused by a new method of order giving. They receive their direction now as suggestions, rather than as pure directives. This leads to a sensation of uneasiness and uncertainty as to the best method of operation. In other words, their sphere of decision making will be very much broadened.

Changes in peer-group relationships will somewhat parallel those with supervisors. Some of his new peers will be old friends (or enemies) who were promoted before him. There will be many strangers with whom he has had no previous contacts. Again, all of them will be eying him as the neophyte and making their own estimates of his chances of survival. The major adjustment the new supervisor will have to make here is in the matter of intensified competition. All supervisors are rivals at their own level for the few advancements open to any of them. This one factor is going to complicate the work of coordination so necessary in the achievement of any manager's goals. Cooperation on the job will be asked and must be given, but behind each act of cooperation will be this underlying competition.

It will be harder for the newcomer to make friends with his peers on a personal basis, but those made will tend to be more permanent and meaningful throughout his business career. His peer group, if properly approached, can be a gold mine of information and useful tips for good operation. Observation of how others operate, without any overt communication, can be very helpful to the newcomer. He will find that ordinarily there is a gentleman's agreement among most members of management that one of their group must not be allowed to look bad to others if this can be avoided. After a decent interval the new supervisor will find himself accepted—either gradually or quite suddenly—as a true member of management, and his peer relationships will tend to simplify.

Some of the heaviest readjustments for the man just promoted to management may be within his own family relationships. No matter how devoted his wife may be or how ambitious she may be for him, she will undoubtedly find it disturbing that her husband now has less time for his family. And, as the chronology often happens, this is often just at the time when the children are most in need of a strong paternal figure. There can be no question that his continued success as a manager will make more demands on his time than he was previously used to on the job. Even if he is physically at home, he will have brought a briefcase full of work with him and will need peace and quiet while he completes his homework. Increased job stresses can quite normally be sublimated by increased tension in domestic relationships. Greater understanding and much deeper forbearance will be demanded of the lady of the house than she has been accustomed to before. Night work, and even the involvement of weekends on the job, will become routine. This is one of the basic facets of the managerial life which must be fully agreed to by both parties if the home life is to be kept on a fairly even keel.

Even the family social life is sure to be radically altered. Time for old friends will be constrained, either by work involvement or by social activities demanded in the new job. While it is true that the family's social circle is likely to be broadened, this may not be in exactly the direction that either the manager or his wife would have chosen for themselves.

A series of promotions usually results in a removal from the old home into "better" surroundings. This uprooting is especially upsetting to teenage children who are bound closely to youthful friendships in school associations. All these forces must be balanced against the family's desire for advancement and improved social and financial position. It will demand deep understanding on the part of each member of the family.

Concentric with all the other changes mentioned will inevitably be a new set of informal social groups. Even if the supervisor continues to bowl or play golf for recreation, it will be in a different league or at a different club. These changes may not even be volitional on the part of the manager, but will seem to be a sort of natural phenomenon.

His wife will become personally involved in quite a different set of clubs and social activities, many of them centered in groups of other managers' wives. One or both members of the partnership will find increasing pressures to take part in more civic activities than they did previously. Most modern companies have strong feelings about involvement of their managers in public work as a necessary part of maintaining the corporate image.

One danger is implicit here—that of letting the tail wag the dog. Initial enthusiasm of the new manager makes it difficult for him to say no when he should. He should always remember that his directly job-related activities are of prime importance and that these peripheral functions must be kept in perspective so that his mental and physical energies can be properly husbanded. It will take his best judgment to maintain correct balance here.

SLOWNESS OF MANAGEMENT DECISION MAKING

The new supervisor makes a discovery shortly after his promotion which gives him much trouble and continues to be a source of difficulty on his job for some time. Before he became a manager, managerial decisions seemed to be produced automatically, either by an omniscient supervisor or by some sort of machine. Irrespective of whether he had agreed with a decision or had violently opposed it, he had not been conscious of any process by which the decision had been made. Now, from his new vantage point, the whole matter of decision making assumes an entirely different face.

In his new position, the supervisor is not particularly surprised that he himself is having trouble in making "foolproof" decisions. His rationalization is that his earlier job had never required any great exercise of this faculty. This is especially true in the area of decisions involving people. But it does come as a real shock to learn that other supervisors also have trouble in making decisions and that there are often long intervals between the recognition of a problem and the final proposal of a solution. This unstructured situation leaves him with a feeling of insecurity that is very troubling to him. Where can he turn to get help in this crucial part of his job if others are experiencing the same difficulty?

Two points are of significance here. The first is that, historically, there has been a dearth of good training in this area until recently, and even yet we have a long way to go before we can claim that there is a really good backlog of training activities in decision making. The second factor is that the realization is slow in coming to the new supervisor that he will *never* find any formula or set of tables which will guarantee him perfect solutions to problems. This is true even in areas that are subject to close quantification—let alone in interpersonal relationships and decisions concerning the people part of the supervisor's job.

If his own supervisors are at all sensitive to his thinking, the new supervisor can find help from them. This will be principally in reducing his anxiety and reassuring him that his trouble is far from unique. In fact, his concern is an indication of one of the first self-developmental activities he must undertake in solidifying his job performance as a member of management.

One of the decisions which a boss must make again and again is a decision about decisions. Many times in his workweek, the first-line supervisor becomes aware that he will be time-pressured and faced with deadlines in many of his necessary decisions. He must then learn to assign priorities to these decisions on a time-lapse basis, always allowing himself the maximum time to work with each problem. He does not have the body of historical data from similar situations which has been accumulated from experience by the older supervisors. For some time while he is new on the job, each decision will represent a situation different in structure from the others he has tackled. Then, of course, as he does begin to accumulate a little experience, he may be led down another fascinating bypath which can be troublesome to him: This is when he will begin to make too-broad generalizations about problems which on the surface appear to be almost identical. It takes real discrimination for him to validate similarities and yet reserve judgment until he has reviewed all available data.

Our new manager does have some sources of help of a generic nature in this situation. There are now some reputable and helpful seminars devoted exclusively to decision making. Simulation models, both with and without help from the computer, are designed as an aid to decision making. The American Management Association has workshops and seminars on the same subject. The Kepner-Tregoe company games are very helpful, and they are designed with long-range follow-up which will keep the student on the track for months to come. (Kepner-Tregoe seminars are designed to train managers at different levels in the hierarchy. By keeping class memberships limited to the same levels, the games can be meaningful to every participant.) Most university schools of business have one or several classes in problem solving, and, in serious situations, some of their staff members are also available as consultants.

One goal must be kept before the supervisor to help him in making his decisions. If he has done his homework properly and has given his very best to arriving at a good decision, he must then lose his fear of being wrong. It is true that to be successful he must bat more than .500. But if he allows the fear of bad decisions to become an obsession with him, he will suffer from "decision paralysis" when he most needs to make them. The duty of his superiors to critique his solutions is clear. This means after the fact, not before the decision is made. The learning situation is reinforced by the comments of the new supervisor's boss, especially if they are given promptly and objectively and are drawn from the bank of experience of the older supervisor.

This activity will build self-confidence in the beginner more quickly than any other exercise. It is the one sure way by which he is most quickly immersed in the atmosphere of managership. From the practical, day-to-day aspect of first-line supervision, his own immediate superior can be most helpful in strengthening his decision-making powers by introducing him as quickly as is practicable into budget construction. Here he must weld "thing decisions" with "people decisions" for the best operation of his part of the enterprise. Since budget construction is always subject to review through many strata of management, he will not be allowed to make any serious errors here which are uncorrectable.

The important point is for the new supervisor and his superiors to work cooperatively to fill what he first feels is a major void in his concept of managership.

MANAGERIAL STYLES AND HOW THE NEW SUPERVISOR SELECTS THEM

Under ordinary circumstances, managerial styles are a reflection of the philosophies of the managers concerned. The conceptual background behind managerial styles can be well summarized in the writings of three people. These are Douglas McGregor, who conceived of "Theory X and Theory Y," and Robert Blake and Jane Mouton, who developed the "Managerial Grid." * One ground rule should be established before going any further: Any description or discussion of managerial *styles* must be kept entirely separate from the results obtained by the manager, unless results (effectivity) are included as a third-dimensional axis in the picture.

McGregor's concept of Theory X and Theory Y represents a polarized situation at the two extremes of a philosophic spectrum. It is an either-or idea. It is unfortunate that Professor McGregor never recorded his concept of "Theory Z" which he is reported to have discussed informally with colleagues and students. This was to have been a much more pragmatic philosophy (and one

---

* Another writer, R. J. Reddin, has begun to attract attention with his ideas on "The 3-D Grid," but so far he has not had the exposure or the acceptance of the earlier writers.

held by a far greater number of managers) which recognized the existence of *both* "good guys" and "bad guys" among the normal population of employees. This would have led quite naturally to a managerial style adjustable to the manager's assessment of each individual employee —that is, on a one-to-one basis. So far as McGregor's influence is concerned, however, it is reflected in the number of ads in the *Wall Street Journal*'s "Mart" section which say the advertisers are looking for prospective employees who operate under Theory Y. It is also sad to note how many managers are still operating from the Theory X position, blithely unaware that there are factors now operant in our society which make this approach completely dysfunctional.

Blake and Mouton, in their two-dimensional pictorialization, with its five major intersections out of a possible 81, have a peculiarly strong appeal to managers with an engineering or technical background. This is perhaps because the system gives the *appearance* of quantification of the concept. The contrasts among the various positions on the grid are great enough to make each one distinct and to call to mind living examples which fit each category quite nicely. Certainly all of us can recall the manager's monotonous refrain, "You gotta get the product outa the door!" which becomes a conditioned response to any given stimulus. Or we can remember with a reminiscent chuckle the manager who (for a very short time) maintained the "country club" atmosphere with a bland disregard for the objectives of the enterprise. The reluctant dragon who breathed fire from his 1-1 position of abdication; "Mr. 5 × 5," who suffered from his pressures in the middle; and the shining white knight, Mr. 9-9, are all familiar enough figures for us mentally to put faces on them. An undeniable asset of the grid concept is its encouragement of introspection by any manager considering the idea. Self-analysis of this sort is always healthy in a manager unless carried to extremes.

It is interesting to watch any group of managers as they are first introduced to the Managerial Grid. Their exercises in placing themselves, their bosses, and their peers on the grid are pursued with glee. They are charmed, and even awed, to discover that their self-placement quite often fits in the center of the cluster of evaluations done by others who know them well. Then, almost inevitably, comes the moment of danger when they begin, unless strongly warned, to associate the posture with the results obtained.

New supervisors should be exposed quickly to some sort of conceptualization of managerial styles. Self-analysis and empirical observation can make an excellent pair of tools to help them toward greater functionalism on the job. Several variables affect the new supervisor's choice of managerial style. In many cases, the supervisor is not aware of, or at least does very little thinking about, these outside influences which shape his behavior. Neither does he examine the matter of style used in a given situation as correlated with his effectivity at the time. It will be worth the time to consider some of these factors in the developing pattern of the new supervisor in his job activity.

Line management. The style of his own manager exerts a tremendous influence on the new supervisor. This may come from "hero worship" or from a calculated or totally unconscious copying of the boss's leadership style. If the boss is inclined to be dynamic and directive, he may overtly state that he wants "things done my way" in his area of supervision. This is a difficult situation to combat, even if the desire is there. One of the greatest frustrations of training and development specialists is to have trainees accept or even become enthusiastic over principles developed in a training series, only to have the trainees return to the line and exhibit no change in behavior because they know that to do so would offend their superior. The result of the manager's influence on his subordinate's style is the same if it comes from the respect and admiration the junior feels for his senior. If the subordinate feels that his manager is especially effective, he can hardly be blamed for a tendency to imitation. The point that is difficult to get across is that a style which one man finds viable may be completely ineffective when used by another person. The matter of managerial style is too closely linked with personality for anything else to be true.

Influence from members of the peer group. Much the same as was said about the boss's influence may be said if the new manager is heavily influenced by friendship with or admiration for other supervisors not in his direct line. One thing different about this situation is that here he is under no direct pressure to adopt any of their methods, and he will do so only if convinced that they are the best. It is interesting, however, to observe that in some organizations there may be "faddism" practiced by members of management in affecting a certain managerial style. This may go so far as to be a heavy factor in determining the atmosphere or working climate of that company. A strong industrial relations superintendent in one plant was completely convinced that the only proper attire for an industrial relations representative was a dark business suit (any color so long as it was blue), a white shirt (with button-down collar), and a bow tie. The reception that greeted his staff in the plant after his edict on dress was implemented was raucous beyond belief. It actually brought labor relations activity by industrial relations personnel to a grinding halt, and nothing productive was accomplished until the ban on sportier clothing was lifted.

Trial-and-error discovery. As the new supervisor becomes aware of the importance of his managerial style, either by intuition or by some of his training, if he is at all sensitive he will probably embark on a series of experimental efforts to discover which style is most functional for his operation. This can be a very disturbing activity, especially as he begins to see the varied reactions he gets from his people as he displays different styles in their work contact. Overreaction to this can occur, with the result that the new manager will clamp on with a death grip to one particular style and refuse to alter it under any circumstances.

Influence of specific training in managerial style. If the new supervisor has any amount of management training these days, he will get some exposure to a discussion of the different sorts of managerial styles. Whether McGregor, Blake and Mouton, Reddin, or anyone else writing in the field is discussed, the same group of managerial styles (under different nomenclature) will appear.

The supervisor who is totally job-oriented to the exclusion of almost all human considerations was the industrial model for many generations in American industry. There are still many anachronistic remnants of his species flourishing today. This is the supervisor operating from McGregor's Theory X or Blake and Mouton's 9-1 position. As a human being, he is no better and no worse than any man around him—it is only in the job situation that he seems to operate with a robotlike, cold efficiency. He is like the schoolteacher to whom his pupils have no sex; his subordinates are not really people, but are tools to help him reach his objectives. This man often achieves great results, from the organizational standpoint. He can become very successful; to some, he will be a model to be emulated down to the last mannerism. His instinct for survival is strong, and those who succeed in staying with him through his ruthless personnel actions may go quite far. It is not surprising that many new supervisors make a calculated decision to pattern themselves after this man; he seems to be traveling the surest —perhaps even the shortest—road to managerial success. What they may fail to realize is that this managerial style, if used consistently, will totally alienate today's crop of industrial workers, whose job mobility is much greater than that of any preceding generation. So long as anything like an expanding economy is with us, this man will no longer be successful, for he still has to get his work done through people.

The supervisor who has abdicated, the don't-rock-the-boater, or Blake and Mouton's 1-1 man is rarely found in American industry, but that doesn't mean that he is imaginary. There are several situations where his operation would be the only practical approach. Included in this category would be the man close to retirement, who is determined to do nothing to jeopardize this goal. He is not about to stick his neck out or assume any risk which might endanger his few remaining years in the work situation. Another who finds this *modus operandi* practicable is the "assistant to," the errand boy and strong right arm of the major executive, whose only reason for being is to implement his boss's instructions. He is the latter-day "special assistant" whose major requirement is "a passion for anonymity." The third place which provides a natural habitat for this manager is in the catacombs of a bureaucracy. Here maintenance of the status quo attains the highest of priorities. This man is basically interested in *neither* the organization nor its employees; his sole purpose is self-preservation in a precarious and vulnerable position. It is comforting to observe that this sort of manager is seldom copied by a new supervisor. His self-seeking qualities are too obvious to all observers; few young men would want to occupy his position.

The third style is deceptive in appearance and is often misjudged by observers. That is Blake and Mouton's 1-9 position or, as they prefer to call it, the "country-club manager." This man is obsessed by his empathy (or sympathy) for people—or at least those people who are working for him. He is so concerned with their welfare and happiness that he has no time to consider the needs of the organization. However, it would be a mistake to conclude that this manager is necessarily a weakling. Some of the strongest leaders in industry tend toward this type of orientation; it is only sad that their strength is employed in a losing cause. Obviously, this kind of man will become expendable to the enterprise whenever the going gets rough financially. Among the first to desert him in times of stress will be his own subordinates, because they can see the untenable position he is occupying. It is reminiscent of the departure from the Garden of Eden to see the defection of his own people from this kind of a manager when they sense that they are in personal danger, and it is even more pitiable to note how stricken this manager is when he realizes what is happening to him.

It was said that a country-club man is not necessarily a weakling. In fact, it takes a sort of strength of character to persist in a course which is so obviously suicidal. He is the prototype of James Branch Cabell's "murderee." Happily, few young managers are attracted to this managerial style. It is usually adopted by a type of personality which in all truth can operate in no other way.

The fourth style is one of the most commonly and most effectively adopted. The "man in the middle" makes a continuing effort to balance with nice calculation his organizational objectives and his treatment of his people. A middle manager is subjected to terrific pressures from below, from above, and from all sides. His job is a continual tightrope walk, and he is successful if his victories are not too obvious and his losses are not too damaging. He is the master of compromise; his genius lies in his ability to reconcile the irreconcilable. Any new supervisor would do well to study this style assiduously. Skill in interpersonal relationships here rates the highest sort of premium, while the necessity for conceptual skills increases year by year and step by step up the hierarchy.

The fifth managerial style is the pot of gold at the end of the rainbow. Here we have Blake and Mouton's 9-9 position or McGregor's Theory Y in full flower. One misapprehension should be corrected about this style. Few managers are ever in a position to operate in this manner for any appreciable time. A prerequisite is almost complete autonomy of operation, and how few of us ever achieve this situation! A few assorted chief executive officers or the fortunate supervisor who is manager of a totally decentralized operation can assume this posture with impunity. All others beware! But the exciting life of the team welded under this manager is a goal for every employee. Creativity is not wished for; it is demanded. Conflict is rampant, and it will be settled by direct confrontation. In every conflict there will be a winner and a loser. But the loser will not spend much time in licking his wounds, because he knows that he has had full opportunity to express his views and to make his arguments. His loss will actually serve as a motivation for even greater effort the next time; his victory then will be all the sweeter. This is participative management in the fullest sense of the concept.

As has been said, if the new supervisor has received

orientation in the area of managerial styles, he will inevitably be examining his own situation to determine which he will adopt under what set of circumstances. This mental exercise, plus the experimentation which will follow, can be one of the most valuable developmental activities of any new supervisor. There must be appended, of course, a searching evaluation of the efficacy of any style tried in its surroundings, with concomitant determination of its validity and reliability.

EFFECT OF STYLES ON PEOPLE, PRODUCTION, QUALITY, AND COSTS

The style or mannerisms of a supervisor will have many subtle effects on the behavior of his employees. If his style is such as to inspire fear or dislike among his subordinates, he can expect reactions from them typical of these emotions. Since the people who make up today's workforce are very mobile, they can move to another job usually with little time loss or major disruption to their lives. Therefore, if they fear or dislike their supervisor, he can expect a continuing high turnover. It is true that, if times are bad, there will be a different result from the hard-driving, overbearing manager who demands production at all costs. Relationships within and between the informal groups will be much more tense under this kind of supervision than under a more permissive leader. Group cohesiveness will be greater because of the increased need for self-protection. The grapevine will be somewhat inhibited, but the rumors flowing along it will be of an extreme nature. The manager who drives his crews hard will often get high production, but he will have more problems in quality than his brother supervisor who is less demanding. Absenteeism and the grievance rate will be noticeably higher in this population than in a group which feels less pressure. Safety records among these people will be below average, and more of them will come to be classified as "accident prone."

Overpermissiveness, however, may result in records not too far different from these, except that production records probably will be poorer. The manager who is totally engrossed in his people problems, to the exclusion of production targets, will find to his hurt amazement that his subordinates are not as appreciative of his sterling qualities as he had expected them to be. On the other hand, once in a while strong informal leadership will arise within this work group and may even result in the accomplishment of organizational goals in spite of the attitudes of the nominal leader. When this happens, it is the result of the personal goodwill of the employees toward their supervisor, rather than the result of his managerial style. Unless this strong, positively oriented informal leadership does appear, this group of employees may have some very sorry records in all areas.

The strong leader in middle management (Mr. 5×5) will have good records in production, quality, costs, labor relations, and so on down the line because he will plan and execute his people's work toward these ends. His managerial style will result in deep commitment from his people, because they recognize an old pro in action and have confidence in the future of their organization under his leadership. This particular managerial style provides the second best climate for good personal development and job enlargement for the employees in it. The new supervisor who finds himself under this sort of leadership is fortunate; he will have excellent chances for growth and promotion if he applies himself and makes the best use of this strong leadership.

The few people who find themselves under the supervision of a man who has autonomy and who is deeply involved with both the organizational goals and the welfare of his people are very fortunate indeed. If they respond normally to this kind of leadership, some spectacular records can be set by the group under any kind of measuring device. Participative management makes full use of the best in every employee, as well as offering incentives for them to reach just a little beyond what they thought was their capacity. The euphoria produced in such a climate is a fine motivator to go on to higher things continually. Any young manager who does have this sort of supervision will find himself spoiled and unwilling for the rest of his working life to operate in any other situation. This is the best developmental environment to be found for any employee, manager or otherwise.

We should stop for a moment to recall that we have been speaking as if a manager always adopts a particular managerial style and thereafter never varies it. This is patently absurd. No situation is ever static for a length of time sufficient for any manager to remain invariant in his operating methods. There will be changes in his management, differences in the company situation, changes in the national or international economy, and comings and goings among his workforce, any or all of which can result in a mix which will make it necessary for him to change his managerial style. These changes should be made from calculated judgment that they are necessary; they should not be made whimsically. Most employees are acute enough to recognize changes which will evoke a different style from their manager, and they will not accuse him of unpredictability if the changes occur for cause.

This is an area in which the new manager should seek frequent counsel from his supervisor. Because his own ego involvement is so high, it becomes almost impossible for him to maintain enough objectivity to make good judgments about this. Actually, the entire matter of the choice of managerial style will start to make a much clearer picture for him when he has been promoted a rank or two and has other supervisors working for him. As is true so many times, he will really learn the most about choice of managerial style when he is teaching it to his subordinates. Because this one aspect of the manager's job has such a strong effect on so many parts of his operation, it becomes one of his most important developmental activities.

TRAINING THE NEW SUPERVISOR

If he is conscientious, the new supervisor will be aware of so many training needs that he will become frustrated. If he doesn't realize these needs, his own manager most certainly will. The cooperation of these two people is mandatory for the best results to be realized.

It goes without saying that by far the greater amount of this necessary training will be received by the new supervisor on the job. He will be subject to continuous counseling from his supervisor, and if his relationships are good, he can gain much stature and grow into his new job more quickly by actively seeking advice and counsel from some of his older and more experienced subordinates, who have seen many bosses come and go.

It is true that this job training will seldom be categorized, either by himself or by others, among the five managerial functions—but it will be there. The biggest mistake the new supervisor can make, and yet one that happens easily, is to get to running so fast that he fails to reserve any time for reflection, evaluation, and proper slotting of the events of his managerial life. One habit espoused by nearly all successful managers is the "quiet time." During this period of each day, no matter what its duration, he must maintain rigid seclusion from interruption by the distracting details of his average workday. This is difficult to do. Some managers find it practicable to do this at the end of the day, when the rest of the people are gone. The only thing wrong with this is that other managers may be following the same custom, and he may have unwelcome interruptions from these men. Some have found it the best procedure to go in early, rather than to stay late. In addition to having fewer people around, they find the time more productive for either reflection or planning because of their fresher physical state.

Formal training. In the average organization, the new supervisor will find a plethora of training provided for him under the formal situation. It is almost universal for him to receive some sort of introduction to and orientation in the job of the manager on a companywide basis. This is ordinarily provided by the training or management development specialists and may total 15 to 40 hours of paid-time training. One of the principal benefits from this ordinarily is a new exposure to key people in other departments and the beginning of a wider understanding of their problems, as well as an invitation to closer contact and liaison with them. In other words, the new manager is invited to start looking at "the big picture."

Most companies also provide training in the fundamentals of supervision, using a variety of approaches and duration. This is not the same look at this area which the new man received in his presupervisory training. It goes more deeply into the fundamentals and also provides some necessary and mundane "nuts and bolts" to facilitate his operations and provide him with some shortcuts.

If his own management is farsighted, he will soon get an opportunity to attend some sort of formal training away from the company. This may be only a two- or three-day seminar, or it might run to several weeks if his supervisor feels he is lacking in a basic body of knowledge best learned in this kind of situation. One of the major advantages of such exposure is his chance to exchange experiences and thinking with people from other companies. This infusion of new concepts will not only suggest possible new methods for his own use, but will also minimize inbreeding of thinking when he remains under the constraints of only his own company's climate.

It must be recognized that a great amount of work is done by the average company in researching training needs for the new supervisor and in course planning and development to satisfy these needs. Right here, however, there may arise one of the most uneconomical aspects of supervisory training. Is it correct, or even nearly so, to assume that all new supervisors will need these segments of training in the same depth and to the same degree? Once they have been established as an integral part of the training arsenal, there is a tendency to force all new supervisors, irrespective of their personal needs, into segments of training of uniform length and uniform presentation. If a particular supervisor does *not* need this area of training, his reaction may be negative toward the whole concept of formal training for a long time to come. Here is the situation that cries for the professional counseling of the management development staff man. His training and judgment in this area will make him better able than even the supervisor's boss to determine in what depth this training is necessary.

Since the transition period is so critical in the development of the new supervisor, the early establishment of this counseling relationship is of the utmost importance.

Actually, it should be a three-way relationship involving the new supervisor, his boss, and the development specialist. Then, too, a fine matter of judgment is involved in determining how much of the new supervisor's time can be spared for formal training when he is so deeply involved in becoming secure in the mechanics of his job.

Self-Development Activities of the New Supervisor

No matter what decision has been made about the amount of formal training the new supervisor should receive, there is no blinking the fact that this time is one in which he dare not neglect the matter of self-development. Early on, the issue was raised that in the last analysis all development work is done by the individual. In spite of the heavy demands on his time, the new supervisor must make provisions for self-analysis and must make use of the counseling of his own manager and the management development specialist to decide what activities he must undertake on his own time to present a better-rounded personality to his job situation.

There are some general categories in which he may expect to need development if his situation is at or near the normal. For example, it is rare that the new supervisor does not need some help in both spoken and written communication. He will become aware of the necessity of communicating orally with classes of people with whom he had no previous direct contact. To all intents and purposes, he will have several new vocabularies (at least the idiomatic ones) to learn. A widely used tool to correct this deficiency is a year or so in a Toastmasters organization. This activity is unique in several ways. Although it has many aspects of a social club, and many lasting friendships can result from this exposure, its principal reason for being is a searching and unremitting atmosphere of criticism of each member's spoken communication. The objectivity of this criticism is maintained at a high level, and every member is subjected to it. Moreover, a Toastmasters club has a well-designed "course" in speech construction which will significantly sharpen a member's incisiveness and clarity of verbal presentation.

Similarly, an off-hour course in written communication, if properly slanted, can be of significant value in sharpening the new supervisor's skill at writing reports and memos. This is one of the most commonly criticized activities of the new supervisor. It seems to make little difference what the educational background of the new supervisor is. Whether his academic education was terminated at high school or whether he is a college graduate, the chances are quite small that he will have spent much time in putting ideas on paper until he entered supervision. Even the one group which is deeply involved in report writing on the job—the engineers and scientists —is notorious for having had poor preparation academically in this important activity. These days the new supervisor is never far from an off-hour course designed to sharpen his written communication. These courses are common in continuing education, community colleges, and universities.

A majority of industrial organizations today recognize the importance of a supervisor's attempts to develop himself by providing company-sponsored tuition reimbursement plans, bonuses for credit completion, and other incentives to help motivate the supervisor to pursue this activity.

One company went so far as to sponsor and run a complete off-hour activity for its supervisors which led to a "Certificate in Management Arts and Science." The curriculum was divided into courses representing human, conceptual, and technical skills. Those who wanted the certificate had to complete eight courses, of which four were "required." The student had a choice of four out of the five subjects: supervisors' management functions, personnel management, financial management and profitability, management science, and group dynamics. The other four subjects could be chosen from a selection of about thirty, which were rotated from quarter to quarter. Normally, it took the candidate from eighteen months to two years to achieve the certificate. The appeal of this program was undeniable, and it is interesting that many of the students already possessed bachelors' or masters' degrees before they even entered the program. In several cases, on the other hand, men who earned the certificate were then motivated to go on to study for an MBA. That the program was meeting a felt need was attested to by its growth. Registration in the first quarter amounted to 237 students; four quarters later, it was up to 819.

The kinds and extent of self-developmental activity will occupy a significant part of the new supervisor's time from here on out. The more quickly he establishes the habit of introspection followed by planned activity, the better prepared he will be to carry on as he enters middle management, which has so many forces militating against developmental activity of any sort.

IMPACT ON THE INDIVIDUAL'S CAREER AND THE
ORGANIZATION'S SUCCESS

It is evident enough by this time that the transition period between being promoted to supervision and arrival at a well-integrated functioning as a working supervisor is crucial to the man's career. This probationary period is the one in which he is subjected to the closest scrutiny and supervision that he will ever receive as a manager. Not only his immediate superior, but many echelons of management above him are keenly interested in his growth and development as a member of management. His performance in the first few months on the job will govern whether he makes it at all, whether he will be judged as a solid first-line supervisor but not likely to be promoted, or whether he will be found to have enough potential to look forward to several promotions during the course of his career.

His contribution to the success of the organization during this transition period will not be inconsiderable. He is at the interface between management and the worker, and it is his responsibility to get his share of the product down the line on time under the best possible conditions of quality and costs. No other member of the enterprise has a heavier responsibility than the first-line supervisor. It would be difficult to overemphasize the importance of establishing many channels of free and open communication at this time. The signals he sends will provide upper managers with the data they need for their long-range decisions; those he receives will be of great assistance to him in the daily conduct of his business.

It would be remiss not to pause here and remind the new supervisor of the importance of his commitment and involvement in the overall success of the organization. Mental activity can never do the whole job; emotion has to enter the picture. Some stimulation of the adrenal glands will be necessary from time to time to boost him over and around the many roadblocks he will find in his way. He will find little time in which to "fall back and regroup" as he gets set in his new management job.

5

The Middle-Management Desert

$\mathcal{S}$o our prospect has been discovered, has been given some presupervisory training, has been promoted to supervision, has made the transition into managership, and has had an indeterminate time in the lower levels of supervision. Hard work, some careful planning, developmental activities, and a little bit of luck have brought him to the attention of upper management, and he has been promoted two or three times. Depending upon the complexity of the organizational structure in which he finds himself, he may be two, three, four, or even five rungs up the ladder when he finally begins to think of himself as in middle management.

The whole term is nebulous in the thinking of most

management people. There is no clear-cut definition or set of standards by which the area of the middle-manager's operation can be definitively limited. We are inclined to think of it more in terms of relative responsibilities and authority, rather than in terms of position in the hierarchy. Even in the same company, this parametric definition can mean that in one department a man could be at the third level of supervision and be well into middle management, while in another department a fourth- or fifth-level manager would still be clearly below the middle-management area. As much as anything else, the evaluation of his peers and his supervisors will categorize a manager as in the middle group.

Another rule of thumb operable in some enterprises is that middle management is said to begin when our manager is promoted into a position where he will be supervising two or more separate subfunctions which may or may not be closely connected in operation. For example, in some businesses the manufacturing and procurement functions may be separate until they join in reporting to the same middle manager.

Still another guidepost used by some is the span of time involved in the manager's decision making. These people state arbitrarily that lower management makes decisions which are implemented in hours, days, weeks, or a few months. When the manager's decisions have a time span of quarters, six months, or a year, this group would designate that he is in middle management. As a matter of fact, all these criteria—plus, of course, the fact that our manager must manage other managers—could be applied collectively to determine that point at which an organization's middle management begins.

Almost all observers agree that the middle manager has responsibilities which consistently outweigh his decision-making authority. His buffering action interfaces between the executive level and the lower levels which supervise the actual production of the product. Yet, in spite of this extremely delicate and important function, the middle manager has little if any policy-making authority. Decisions he makes by the dozens; policy he makes only in the case of default at the executive level.

For these reasons, it is not surprising that his general reactions are quite conservative. He has a great personal stake in maintaining the status quo. It therefore follows quite logically (in his thinking) that he often becomes a communication block both upward and downward in the chain of command. He knows from experience that many things will disappear if he leaves them long enough in his "hold" basket. This can even go so far as the implementation of new policy sent down from mahogany row with which he does not agree. His actions seem to be more machiavellian than they actually are.

Yet, in spite of all the foregoing, if significant change is to be effected within an organization, the middle manager will have more to do with it than will any other echelon of management. He has at his command the elements and facilities which will make this change possible with a minimum of friction from all concerned. Executive levels are too far removed from the firing line to be effective as direct change agents. They must, perforce, rely on their lieutenants to carry out this part of the process. Another aspect of middle managers' solid value to the company's welfare is their store of experience and well-oiled habits of decision making. By intuition, it seems, they are able to stabilize the day-to-day operation of the enterprise throughout its sometimes sudden changes in production, its periodic ups and downs in quality performance, and its shorter or longer periods of difficulty with cash flow or profit squeezes.

It is observable that many talented managers reach

a plateau in middle management. Their rewards are substantial in money, power, and prestige. If effective, they have a great amount of respect from both subordinates and superiors, and they may make the calculated decision that the rarefied atmosphere of the next step into the executive level is not worth the extra sacrifices demanded. Even here, then, there may be a tendency toward a perpetuation of conservatism. A manager can make a fine career for himself in middle management, and he can remain there with no sacrifice to his ego or self-actualization needs if he so desires.

However, if his ambition is still hot or is even made hotter by his closer exposure to the executive level, his sojourn in middle management can be extremely frustrating and stultifying to our manager. Middle management is the desert of the management field.

The Neglected Man in the Management Field

From the standpoint of management development, the man in the middle would seem to have been forgotten by everyone, including himself. At this time in his career, months and years can slip by with developmental activity submerged under a flood of job details. As a manager of managers, he will see to the development of his subordinates from self-protective instincts if for no other reason. He knows that he himself is not about to move up until there is a qualified replacement for his own position, and preferably two. But, somehow, his own needs in this area become easy to overlook. This peculiarity of the middle manager is almost universal; it is not limited to any particular business or industry.

It is easier to understand why this may happen if we take a look at the unbelievable pressures to which he is subjected on the job. From below come pressures of young, avid managers hot on the trail of their own advancement, no matter what the cost. Their interest in job enlargement and the acquisition of greater responsibilities may be either genuine or spurious; its effect on the time of the middle manager is the same no matter what the motivation of the middle manager's subordinates. In many cases, the middle manager will be supervising young managers who are thrown into situations which are purely competitive. Their maneuvering for advantage is especially trying on the middle manager because of his unquestionable need for all the objectivity at his command in resolving the conflicts which will result. Actually his position here is much more than that of a mere referee. In some situations, he will be forced to take a position for one of the competitors and against the other. This will complicate his interpersonal relationships and make more necessary continuing evidence of his essential objectivity.

The pressures coming from above are more onerous than the middle manager has ever been subjected to before. As the buffer for the executive level, he is the one charged with the implementation of policy decisions. Because of the impact of these decisions on the whole enterprise, the weight of this responsibility can be crushing. Then, too, after handing him this delightful little package, executives have a way of withdrawing into Olympian unapproachability and leaving him as the only available contact for those involved in the rest of the organization. His accountability is much more direct than it was earlier in his career, too, and is much more frequently reviewed with him.

Unfortunately for him, the middle manager is the butt of some vicious company politics. Competition at the executive level is for real and for keeps. The stakes are too large for anyone to be uninterested. In this connection, the middle manager has two choices, neither of them particularly enviable. He can *try* to maintain a position of complete and total neutrality, thereby inviting more approaches for the enlisting of his support. Or he can momentarily evade this sort of pressure by "choosing sides" with one of the contestants or one clique. More about this gambit later.

In his role as an aspirant for an executive position, the middle manager is directly under the gun 24 hours of each day. Neither on nor off the job can he escape constant evaluation by his superiors, and this aspect of his trial will invade even his social or private life. Executives have not arrived at their positions without becoming expert in exerting pressure. It is recognized in most companies as a regular part of the executive selection procedure.

But even with all this, the heaviest pressures to which the middle manager is subjected will come from his peers. The narrower the part of the pyramid they inhabit, obviously the fewer the roosting spots that remain available. The game of musical chairs becomes grimmer and more exacting at each higher level in the hierarchy.

Peer group pressures can be applied in an endless number of ways. Have you ever joined with a group in applying the game of oversolicitude about a colleague's health? Even if he *knows* what is going on, it takes a strong character to resist the subtle doubt as to his own well-being. Gamesmanship must have been invented by a group of middle managers in their pack-hunting forays. The innuendo, the character-assassination, the guilt by association, the damning with faint praise, the cloak-hidden rapier thrust—all are "fair" weapons on the middle-management battleground.

Even if their intent is not lethal, the pressures of

peers may not be any the lighter. Coordination and liaison work at this level are of overwhelming importance to the achievement of objectives, and here we are talking about the objectives of the whole enterprise, not just a small or insignificant part of it.

In his adjustment to this whole picture, it is not surprising if the middle manager becomes a little neglectful of his own personal growth. He is too concerned with protecting what he has already achieved to become very conscious of the more leisurely and concentrated efforts involved in self-betterment. Again we come back to the necessity of maintaining the status quo, which looms so large in the thinking of any man at this stage of his business career. It boils down to the fact that his ability to keep centered on this need is another of the selection criteria applied to any middle manager who still wants to advance.

There is another reason why the man in the middle may be the subject of developmental neglect. Everyone assumes by this time that he is a real pro, himself not excepted. He has been making decisions of importance to the enterprise for years, with observable success. He has gained the confidence of both his superiors and his subordinates, and he has let them down few times so far in his career. His experiences on the firing line of first-level supervision gave him the confidence necessary for advancement, since these decisions were implemented quickly and results could be checked within a matter of hours or days.

He has become intimately familiar with all the involutions of his organization; it is almost impossible to surprise him about anything in operations in his area. Subsequent to his arrival in middle management, he has had more and more occasions to develop his conceptual abilities as his manager has given him bigger chunks of the operation as his personal responsibility. His total experience has contributed immensely to his maturation. His continued success would not have been possible had not an aura of trust grown up among his superiors, his subordinates, and his peers. Everyone feels that this man can be trusted to take an assignment and work it to a successful conclusion.

This is all very fine. But what of the dynamics of his total environment? Is he positive, through repeated checkings, that he has stayed abreast of new technical developments in his field? How long has it been since he and his boss formally evaluated his developmental progress? Even if he has made a reasonable effort to escape technical obsolescence, what of the more subtle and complex advances in the behavioral sciences which can increase his effectiveness in his interpersonal relationships if he masters them and adapts them to his use?

What this means is that, if he relies too heavily on his image as an old pro, he may become insensitive to his own needs for personal development. Because these needs are hidden from everyone concerned, or at least are not observed, they are the more insidious in the damage they can do as they accumulate. Just as by this time in his physical life he should be getting regular checkups from his doctor, so he should formalize a procedure for checking on his personal growth with his superior and the management development staff specialist. This now becomes a purely consultative type of relationship, since each program must be individually tailored. More will be said of this again.

The old-pro concept militates against the effectiveness of his incoming channels of communication. Both his subordinates and his superior by this time will be saying, "We certainly don't have to tell George this! He's known all about it for years." Who says so? Just maybe George *doesn't* know this little tidbit, and just maybe he might think it important to his operations.

In one sense, the old-pro concept is inimical to any personal growth at all. The middle manager has become accustomed to being called upon as an expert in his own area of work, in the company at large, and perhaps in the field of management itself. Depending upon his own personal characteristics, he may by this time be doing quite a bit of speaking here and there at the request of outside agencies. This is excellent in helping him to crystallize and verbalize his personal philosophy, but it is not particularly conducive to a vigorous and healthy personal growth. For every time he speaks in public, he should also listen at least once to the ideas of other (and strange) managers.

However, it is true that by this time his own professionalism as a manager should be well-rooted. His position is very nearly that of a country doctor who has gained the complete confidence of the patients in his area and who is, undeniably, competent. But this same general practitioner is well aware that his knowledge is far from sufficient in some of the more obscure troubles he sees, and he will turn without hesitation to the specialist for help here. He will also probably schedule himself every year or two for a month in some medical center where he can absorb at first hand the new medical developments. In other words, our country GP is practicing a good kind of personal development which our middle manager would do well to emulate.

A big contributor to this whole problem is that much of the glamour and some of the challenge have gone from his job. When he was at the bottom of the ladder he was strongly pushed by his personal ambition to prove, both to himself and to others, that he was indeed a better man than his position indicated. Then, when he did advance into the middle-management area, once more he had a new and fresh challenge with which to grapple. The bigger job demanded more muscle, more concentration, and better performance than before. But, in subduing these new problems, he was faced with a much longer wait for one of the few vacancies to occur which could lead to a promotion into the executive level. With the passage of time, it would be inevitable that a little "ho hum" might appear once in a while in the fringes of his consciousness. This mental slowdown, with concomitant complacency, can be the ruin of a good man unless he actively fights the encroachment of such attitudes into his thinking.

The Beginning of Isolation

Ever since he became a supervisor, our middle manager has been aware at times that he is alone. He is alone during the decision-making process. He is alone whenever there is discipline to administer. He is alone whenever he implements a change within his group. He is alone in the self-evaluation he must do periodically to determine his progress or lack of it. But in these situations his aloneness is as much a matter of choice as it is of being forced upon him. Self-reliance at these times is a must.

When we speak of isolation, however, one or two other factors may enter the picture. A manager conceivably might isolate himself deliberately for a short period of time. This might be a defensive measure to maintain his objectivity during times of extreme pressures from those about him. One would expect that these times would be relatively far apart and of short duration. The other possibility is that he is becoming isolated without even being aware of it.

The middle manager has direct superior-subordinate relationships with relatively few other managers, but he has direct working relationships with several layers in the managerial hierarchy. This is unavoidable, nor would it be desirable to avoid it. His progression up the line has removed him from direct contact with the actual production of the company's product, except in those rare cases when he decides on a personal tour of inspection. Even when he makes these, if he is sensitive to the feelings of his subordinates he will refrain from many personal contacts lest his managers feel that he is bypassing them. As this pattern emerges, he is insulated from many cues he formerly received and must depend more and more for his feel of the enterprise's health upon the information he receives through the chain of command. We all know how a message may be distorted through this kind of communication by the personal bias of every instrument used in the process. It then becomes possible for a middle manager to be comfortable in the possession of large amounts of incomplete or distorted operating information.

Another factor which may compound the encroachment of isolation is his heavy concentration on the flow of information and directives he receives from the executive level. His own input to the downward transmission of those parts of the communication he decides to send will apply the same bias and distortion to his messages as is applied to the messages he receives from below.

Whatever management training our middle manager has received has repeatedly reinforced his need for proper delegation to subordinates. His own working days are immensely crowded and busy. His subordinates, his supervisor, and many peers are continually competing for his time to take care of all necessary interfaces. He has discovered that this mass of minutiae has made it necessary for him to hire one or more staff assistants in addition to his direct line subordinates in order to keep his head above the flood of work. Every time another subordinate is added, proportionately less of his time remains discretionary to him. In other words, another little slice from the pie of his day's span has been whittled away. At the very least, the sum total of these factors will result in an insulating wall being erected between our manager and the real world, if not total and complete isolation. As was said, this process is so gradual that the man may be totally unaware of how far he is out of contact with the firing line.

It can be argued that this is his fault if it is allowed to happen. It is his duty to devise and install enough of the sorts of controls that will make this situation impossible. Unfortunately, our middle manager is as human as the next man, and he may read his reports and interpret his control data to suit his own desires, rather than seeing exactly what they are telling him.

We might be permitted the luxury of asking in all seriousness how much our superintendent *really* knows of his own area. Geographically, it may be quite large. He may have reporting to him, through all channels, several hundred to a thousand or more people. More than one function will probably be represented. If the enterprise is concerned with the manufacture of a product, a second and even a third shift may further separate him from direct contact with a major part of the activity. Except for tie-ins of only a few moments' duration, these other shifts operate effectively as separate entities, at least so long as there is no apparent major problem in their area.

Business management is replete with prime examples of this sort of isolation. In one case, a production superintendent in an aluminum reduction mill was vaguely aware that the plant's consumption of copper in the "flexes" used in the Niagara pots was becoming quite excessive. A spot-check showed that "burnoffs" or losses of carbon anodes owing to overheating of the flex was fairly high. A little closer analysis revealed that these were far from accounting for all the copper usage. The superintendent was then thoroughly alarmed, and he launched an investigation with the help of industrial relations through its security unit. The final outcome was the embarrassing discovery that for more than a year a "ring" of thieves on the second and third shifts had been systematically stealing copper and disposing of it through a dishonest local junk dealer. Total losses to the company amounted to more than $75,000. This superintendent, in his younger years as a first-line supervisor, had been exceptionally perceptive within his area and had maintained a beautiful network of communications with his people. In talking about this incident, the superintendent admitted that a major portion of his chagrin over the happening was the indisputable evidence that he had lost touch with his people.

In another plant in the same company, a promising young man had been hired on college graduation as a labor relations representative. His flair for the work was so great and his effectiveness was so high that he became industrial relations superintendent within five years, before he was quite thirty. He had been meticulous in maintaining a communications network with both line management and the union officers and grievance men. However, a recent union election had resulted in the elevation of a new chief grievance man. One night the superintendent was apprised at 11 P.M. by his second-shift labor relations man that there was imminent danger of a wildcat strike at the beginning of the third shift over an unsettled grievance about some work assignments. The superintendent talked with his representative for about ten minutes, then instructed him to tell the chief grievance man that there could be no condoning a wildcat and to ask him to come to the superintendent's office at eight o'clock in the morning. The men did go out at midnight, all the pots froze for lack of an orderly shutdown, and the hard-dollar loss to the company was more than $5 million. The young superintendent had allowed himself to become isolated from one of his best sources of information.

More recently, in another industry, the top executives had become convinced that in a boom economy new employees would no longer respond (through fear of job loss) to the hard-nosed managerial style which had been practiced for many years within the company. They thereupon began an intensive communication-training series with their management on paid time which centered mainly about the newest behavioral science activity in employee motivation. All levels of management personnel took this training. As might be expected, there was a broad spectrum of behavioral change (or lack of it) after the training had been completed. About a year later, during a period of rapid expansion in the workforce, one of the area superintendents became alarmed over his group's consistently high rate of voluntary attrition over several months. The superintendent asked that a survey be done within his area to determine if possible what trends were leading to this high attrition figure.

Two factors appeared loud and clear. Exit interviews with the voluntary quits repeatedly elicited the feeling that management considered them something less than human beings. They felt no sense of any consideration for their human dignity when they came in contact with members of management. The second factor was a clear-cut indication from supervisors that their signal from their area management was "business as usual" instead of the changed approach to employees advocated in the training just received. In fact one third-level supervisor had just been transferred to another area because of his "coddling of his people." This area superintendent was clearly in total isolation both from the signal being given by company executives and from the inputs coming up the line from his own subordinate managers.

The middle manager who has any consideration for his future must be constantly on guard against evidences of this kind of isolation. The farther he goes up the ladder, the greater his need for sensitivity to what is going on about him. The higher he goes, the more delicate will be the cues he receives from those about him, and he will be required to maintain greater alertness. No man can operate in a vacuum; each is very much dependent upon his observation of his fellow workers and his necessary response to their attitudes and actions.

THE CONSTRICTION OF TIME AND WORK PRESSURES ON PERSONAL DEVELOPMENT

It is at this point in his career that the manager may be in danger of letting his job manage him. Pressures of time and job detail become fantastic. No matter how hard he runs, he seems to gain not an inch on the road toward mastery of his job. Everyone with whom he has contact on the job contributes to this scramble. His superiors, his peers, and his subordinates are busily whittling at his personal time and decreasing his ability to reserve any of it for personal reasons. He is made to feel grossly selfish if he undertakes any activity which is not connected directly with achievement of the organizational objectives.

Ultimately, he has no one to blame for this but himself. In a sense, if he allows this situation to develop, it is an indication of a sort of inverted egoism. He begins to imagine himself the indispensable man. One of the very first self-developmental activities he should undertake at this point is a strengthening of his ability in delegation.

For the most part, however, his time pressures develop quite naturally from the scope of his job and his personal dedication to it. By this time, his ego-involvement in the organism he has largely created himself is too great to admit of any abdication from its care and feeding. His line relationships, if the organization is normally stable, have for some time been solidified into a small, tight group of several years' standing. There have been few changes in personnel, especially in the line directly above him, and their evaluation of his ability and performance has also solidified into a concept subject to change only from some great or suddenly visible variation. These are not likely to occur. Also, during this time he is being subjected to the most rigorous kind of management by results. If his objectives meet the tests of consonance with the larger organizational objectives and have the blessing of his immediate supervisor, he has only to meet these to emerge in good shape from either formal or informal performance evaluation. What is commonly overlooked is the question of how much more spectacular his successes might have been had he not allowed conscious attention to developmental activities to be submerged under his daily work regimen. No one ever knows the true capacity of a champion until he has been fully extended, and someone must do this deliberately—either his boss or himself.

If the full truth were told, many of the pressures upon his time are delusive or are at least the product of poor time planning on his part. The application of some of the rudiments of work simplification to his own job may prove embarrassingly illuminating. A significant portion of the activities involved in the workday of a middle manager may be found under close scrutiny to be of a pleasant variety but not essential to the success of his business venture. It becomes easy to convince oneself that those long "business" lunches or golf matches *really* have all that much to do with the success of the business.

There has already been mention of how important it is to establish and maintain the habit of a daily quiet time. If this does not become a completely ingrained part of the middle manager's daily routine, he will be missing one of his best opportunities for the continuing introspection essential as a forerunner to well-considered developmental activities. The first essential in reaching a goal is to determine our present position with relationship to that goal. This of itself will be one of the large determinants of developmental methodology. Let us say, for example, our middle manager is convinced that to make any real enlargement of his job sphere he is going to have to become a more effective oral communicator. This communication is at a level where considerable finesse is demanded if it is to be effective. Therefore, one of his most closely related job activities might be the acceptance of a major chairmanship in the local Chamber of Commerce, where the need for considerable powers of persuasion is magnified many times.

It may be true that time pressures have submerged a middle manager's self-developmental work; it does not follow that this is necessarily inevitable.

LACK OF ADEQUATE FEEDBACK MECHANISM

Another factor which works against proper self-developmental activity of the middle manager is the aforementioned shell of isolation growing about him. Any introspective exercise is largely dependent upon the efficiency of the feedback loops surrounding the man. In the case of the middle manager, these have become distorted. Filters have been superimposed by himself, by his subordinates, and especially by his peers. These filters are for the most part designed for self-protection of his associates, with no real regard for the explicit function of a feedback loop. Unless feedback is objective and truthful, its final effect will be harmful rather than wholesome.

The middle manager can be deluded by the apparent simplicity and tightness of his formal organizational structure. He reassures himself that his network of communication extends to every portion of his area and that his subordinates have developed strong loyalty through their association with him. This is true up to a point. However, this man is far enough from the actual happenings on the production line that anything his subordinates think undesirable for him to know is fairly easy to bury.

The manager's own image in his people's perception can be far different from that which he visualizes. He may be admirably clear and incisive in his own downward communication, only to have the message that is received on the line be 180 degrees out of phase with his intended message.

The best defense against this is a well-planned and conscientiously executed personal spot check on a random basis by the manager himself. The assessment of morale in a working group is accomplished by both communication and simple observation. When done by the manager, these, plus an evaluation of certain recognized indicators such as productivity, quality, costs, grievance rate, and safety performance, can give him a picture which will not be too far from the actual truth—if he is willing to take the trouble.

Our middle manager will, in this same connection, do well to pay particular attention to the functioning of the informal groups within his organizational structure. The old timers, irrespective of their position in the formal line, often have extremely high status and esteem among their fellow workmen. Their considered opinion of the boss and his operations can have a very strong effect upon his picture in the organization. B. M. Bass has postulated the existence of three kinds of leadership: imposed, assumed, and effective.* Either imposed or assumed leadership can be effective only with the acceptance of the followers. One of the better ways for a middle manager to insure effectiveness of his leadership is to cultivate good relationships with leaders of the informal groups. Their influence can multiply his many times throughout the organization. Also, the feedback which the manager receives from the informal leaders is much more likely to be free from personal bias than is the feedback he gets from line subordinates, who have a much heavier ax to grind.

This matter of the establishment and maintenance of good feedback loops is of critical importance to the middle manager, and it will become even more so if he is later promoted to an executive position. The sum of the information received from this source will be his best

---

*B. M. Bass, *Leadership Psychology and Organizational Behavior,*. Harper & Brothers, New York, 1960.

signal as to the areas in which he needs to spend the most time on his personal development.

THE HALO EFFECT AND THE WAGON-AND-STAR MECHANISM

It has been said that a corporation is the elongated shadow of one man. The same can be said of the executive responsible for a major portion of an enterprise. As he designs and builds his organization, he will choose a hard core of trusted lieutenants who will carry most of the burden in the running of his segment of the business. As he gains his reputation, much of it rubs off on these subordinates simply from their association with the leader. It is possible for one or more of these subordinate managers to gain reputations quite a bit in excess of their actual ability to deliver, from this halo effect gained from their juxtaposition to the executive.

This halo effect will operate to some extent in the minds of the neutral observers and usually to a larger extent in the thinking of the manager himself. The stronger the leader he is, the more difficult it is for him to believe that his subordinates are anything less than supermen. Part of this is simple reinforcement of his original choice of subordinate personnel. The remainder comes from the fact that his organization has been successful, and, as the old saying goes, it is hard to argue with success.

The second echelon of managers under a particularly strong leader may go for years from apparent success to apparent success without ever having had their own abilities tested in real depth. This is because their leader has not allowed them to make a serious mistake which would reflect on his organization. This is made more visible sometimes when one of these lieutenants is promoted away from his protector and put into a position where he must stand on his own feet. The sudden realization of his new exposure and vulnerability may of itself cause a severe reaction in the man which will work against his success. He may either freeze or spin his wheels in a public exhibition of futility very damaging to the success of his group.

The manager who allows this to happen to the men reporting to him is negating the very fundamentals of management development. No man will develop far or strongly when he is deliberately kept in a position of dependency. Like any other immature person, he will take his share of bumps and falls while he is learning to walk in the management world, but he must learn to walk before he can ever run. The possessor of a halo whose source of illumination is the reflected glory of a brilliant boss must be tough-minded enough not to allow his own thinking to be clouded. He will have to maintain constant surveillance of his own developmental progress by introspection. He can learn many valuable things from this sort of supervision, but his own personal survival and progress will still depend entirely upon his own powers of observation and self-analysis.

The "wagon and star" mechanism is similar to the situation just described, except that in its pure sense it results from a deliberate action on the part of the subordinate. He makes a choice of a hero with whom he casts his lot for better or for worse. We have all seen many instances where a man or a group of men have attached themselves like barnacles to a strong and upwardly mobile manager. Their immediate success from this ploy may be quite spectacular. If their boss is jet-propelled up the managerial ladder, they will also be dragged along like the tail of a comet. This sort of career development is especially noticeable in a young and growing firm or in one which makes use of the project type of organization. In the latter, the strong man will be chosen as a project manager. Within a short time, the observer can see the cadre begin its formation. One after the other, the old lieutenants are picked up and assume their new positions in the project under their old leadership. It should not be inferred that this is necessarily a bad procedure. It is a natural thing for a man to pick as trusted subordinates those who have performed well for him in the past.

The danger to the subordinate manager in this procedure lies in the political field. In middle management and above, politics becomes one of the biggest dangers to managers. By entrusting their entire future to this star above them, they themselves become directly affected by his political success or lack of it. Their complete loss of identity in the aura of their boss makes them subject to rising or falling in direct relationship to his success or failure.

If a manager is normally intelligent and has his share of expertise in interpersonal skills, he will have a better chance of long-range success if he is known by others to be his own man rather than in a position of blind followership of another man, no matter how brilliant that man may be. With rare exceptions, the manager will have a better career if he passes through the supervision of a number of superiors. If nothing else, from these different people he will have a variety of experiences which will make him a better-rounded individual. This whole matter, of course, revolves about the continuing struggle in American industry between individualism and conformity. The question in any manager's mind is, "When and how much do I deviate from the accepted norms of the managerial group?" Creative innovation can occur only from deviant action; it requires maturity of judgment to recognize the climate in which this action has a reasonable chance for success.

CONVENTIONAL MIDDLE-MANAGEMENT TRAINING AND DEVELOPMENTAL ACTIVITIES

From the emphasis that has been put on the over-all lack of concentration on developmental activity for the middle manager, it might be inferred that nothing in the way of development ever occurs in the middle-manager's life. This is not really true. But, even when some type of developmental activity is initiated, there is a curious lack of imagination or creativity in the ventures undertaken. In many cases, they are repetitious of developmental activities he has already undergone since becoming a manager, rationalized and sugar-coated by claims for "greater depth" and "wider scope," neither of which can as a rule be substantiated. A look at some of the typical developmental activities for the middle manager might emphasize what has been said here.

Middle-management seminars. There are literally hundreds of seminars held each year by universities, management associations, and management consultants which lure the middle manager with broad-brush promises of great enlightenment on his job and of enrichment of his capabilities. With a few notable exceptions, these are merely a rehash of the management theory with which the manager has been working for years. Of course, he may get some good from the change of pace and the change of scene, but if he is normally acute he is bound to come away feeling short-changed. If this happens to him two or more times, it is predictable that he may have a reaction against the whole idea of management training. It

is desirable that he check with the management development specialist in his own company before making a
choice of such a seminar activity. There are some good
ones, and he should be especially careful to pick one of
these.

Job rotation. The name "job rotation" has a nice,
satisfying sound to the average executive when he is counseling his subordinates on their personal development.
Upper management may even go so far as to set up an
elaborate network of positions whose incumbents are rotated on a fixed schedule. There is a major flaw in such
an exercise. When it becomes too routinized, everyone concerned knows that there is no real accountability given to
a job holder who will be there only a few months. The
process degenerates into a glorified and extended visit,
rather than an actual job. Someone else will actually be
carrying the responsibility for the area. It is true that
even this process will enlarge somewhat the perspective
of the middle managers involved in the carousel ride,
but there can be nothing like the results hoped and claimed
for this activity.

It is most certainly true that the fundamental concept of job rotation is sound. Especially if our manager
has come straight up the line in one function, he should
be ready to gain a great deal from exposure in other areas
than his own. But, to be meaningful, these assignments
should be of indefinite duration and should give the manager full and total job responsibilities for whatever position he may be occupying at the time. There is further advantage here in having a look at a variety of types of supervision, rather than being locked in the line with which
he has become familiar.

Another common mistake made in the network type
of rotations is that in a great majority of cases, all the
moves are made on a lateral basis. If some real planning

is done, the middle manager's job rotation should be done upward on the spiral staircase. Self-contained in this concept would be the necessity of documenting the manager's capability before sending him on to the next and higher position. By this time, our manager is on the threshold of the altitude where "a manager is a manager is a manager." That is, he is in the area where the function of the organization he is managing is not really germane. By this time, he should be able to make the transition from department to department, or even from industry to industry, with only a minimal time necessary for readjustment to the new enterprise and its vocabulary.

Coaching by superiors. If the middle manager's own supervisor is conscientious and has even the slightest amount of insight, one-to-one coaching in the job situation can be a tremendous boost to any man's development. The trouble is, of course, that both the manager and his boss are too likely to succumb to everyday work pressures, with the result that coaching deteriorates into nothing but post-mortems on the more glaring booboos perpetrated by the subordinate. No man is going to learn much from his clinkers if he is put immediately into a defensive posture as soon as one has been discovered.

Community relations activities. A great deal of self-satisfaction is derived by some executives from sheer numbers of their middle management who are gaining visibility as loaned executives to United Good Neighbors, as advisers to Junior Achievement clubs, or as members of the local school board. The fatal fallacy here is again ordinarily a lack of follow-up. Such positions as discrete compartments in the life of the middle manager carry intrinsically very little transfer of learning. They make up another facet to his personal life, but unless some conscious effort is put into a study of the experience, he will be unlikely to relate it to his job life.

WHAT DOES MANAGEMENT OWE TO THE MIDDLE MANAGER IN DEVELOPMENT?

The greater part of this chapter has been devoted to laying out the many roadblocks and difficulties which lie in the way of the proper development of the middle manager. Some of these are caused by the manager himself, some by the attitudes of his supervisors, and some by the very nature of the job itself. But, if we are going to assure ourselves of a proper flow of executive candidates, we must manage these difficulties and keep the middle manager in a smooth and continuing development process. The responsibility of management in this situation is very real and quite clear-cut. There are several things which must be kept on the agenda if we are to achieve this goal.

Keeping the middle manager alert. If, in the pressure of his duties, the middle manager becomes a trifle lax in his own self-developmental regimen, his supervisor owes it to him to agitate the matter at regular intervals. The easiest way for this to be done is to maintain calendar dates for performance reviews on a formal basis. This will be an automatic reminder once or twice a year and will make it impossible for our man to keep slipping his developmental schedule until the habit is established. An executive who keeps the proper development of his subordinates as a primary goal for himself will quite naturally work some references to potential development action into his day-to-day coaching, as well as into the formal reviews. This will keep both the boss and the subordinate headed in the right direction.

Real development activities. The superior owes to his subordinate the courtesy of helping him to develop a growth program with some real meat and meaning to it. This should be the most frequent point of contact with the management development specialist, whose training and work make him especially qualified to give advice on these matters. There must be both a sense of urgency and a real commitment by the manager to the program. The idea of self-development, along with an awareness of current developmental activities, must never be far from the consciousness of our middle manager.

Supportive attitude. Beleaguered as he is by pressures from every direction, the middle manager must be continuously aware of support and comfort given to him by his superior if he is going to maintain a significant rate of growth. Not that his superior will do the job for him, nor would he if he could; but the encouragement and the moral support must never be absent. This aura of support is one of the reasons why the home team always has the advantage in an athletic contest.

Time and financial support. Basically requisite to a complete developmental program for the middle manager is enough released time and enough money from the company to enable him to afford the items which he has planned and documented as necessary to his proper growth. If it has been properly determined that our middle manager could derive great benefit by taking formal programs, then there must be no question about making arrangements for absences of three months, six months, or nine months if these are the stated lengths of the programs. Neither must he be allowed to suffer any sort of financial loss from having undertaken a developmental activity. Absence at a formal management seminar can never be construed as an excuse for passing over a merit increase if it falls due during the manager's absence.

Proper irritation and stretching. Part of management's responsibility to its middle managers is to see that their job situation can never deteriorate into repetitious and boring routine. At all times, every manager must be faced with challenge sufficiently great to keep him stretched and taut. This in itself will insure a certain amount of growth, as well as keeping the middle-manager's mentality alert and active.

Honesty in communication. The middle manager, because of his strategic position in the hierarchy, should be a well-informed man. But we have already seen how it can be possible for his "information" to be either incomplete or downright inaccurate. His superiors owe him honest and complete communication in everything that pertains to the job situation. Their integrity, as well as his, is dependent upon a free, honest, and accurate flow of the information pertinent to his job.

*   *   *

Apart from the fact of having been chosen for supervision in the first place, the period of time spent in middle management is the most critical in the work history of any manager. If his progress and earlier growth have been fairly normal, the manager has a good chance of entering middle management in his late thirties or early forties. This means that more than half of his employment career still lies ahead of him. Whether he lives from here on out in this (in many ways) pleasant and rewarding plateau or whether he goes on to greater responsibilities is the end product of many different forces. At no time before or later in his career has his amount of self-determinism been smaller. It is therefore all the more urgent that the middle manager devote every available ounce of energy to keeping his personal growth and maturity at the optimum. Of course, in the last analysis the only real responsibility for this is his own.

6

The Second Selection Process

THE search for potential executive timber by
top management is much more intensive and more closely
followed than is the effort made to find potential supervisors from the general population. This is understandable, since executives are of course subject to much
more scrutiny at all levels within the company. This is
not to say that it is impossible for a major gaffe to be
made because of attitudes toward a chief executive. More
than once in the history of American business, no con-
certed search was made for a successor to the big boss
simply because no one could face the possibility of his
death or retirement. If he has been an especially strong
president, a paralysis can overtake the mental processes
of all concerned in the matter of naming an heir apparent.
This attitude, it must be said, is also sometimes exhibited
by the man himself.

However, in any company large enough to have more than one echelon clearly recognizable as executive in caliber, some sort of executive search and recognition methods will be used. The sad part of the whole matter is that this area has consistently shown some of the most haphazard methodology of the business world. One would sometimes think that we are still in the 19th century as we look at some companies' efforts to find backup men for their executive corps.

How Do We Recognize the High-Potential Manager?

The variety of ways by which lower- or middle-management people are tabbed as "comers" is as great as the personal idiosyncrasies of the top management concerned. Many strong entrepreneurs make a fetish out of their ability to make instantaneous decisions. This means that it is possible for the very fleetest of impressions to result in a young man's being included in the list of those subject to special attention. A quick answer, a well-turned phrase, a happily remembered statistic conceivably may have a tremendous effect on the life of a young man if a listening executive happens to be in an impressionable mood.

Many companies are famous (or notorious) for picking executive timber by a process of type casting. For many years, one company picked all its executive trainees from among the graduates of a particular West Coast university. Immediately after a change in company presidents, it became noticeable that now the graduates of one of the Ivy League schools were the front runners. In some companies, usually the smaller ones, religion may be a determinant of a place among the elect.

As we have already noted, it is not impossible for a

man to achieve an executive position as a rider on the coattails of his boss and protector. Pragmatically, it might be argued that this is not an altogether indefensible posture, since it is highly probable that a successful executive will surround himself with subordinates in whom he recognizes certain necessary strengths.

The executive in search of a replacement is always on dangerous ground when he allows personal biases to have a determining strength in his decision making about executive replacement. There are at least two reasons why this is a hazardous practice. First, bias of this sort can perpetuate or even augment weaknesses in the executive group if the same weaknesses are present in the incumbents. It is a human characteristic for us to ignore, or even completely fail to see, weaknesses in others if they are the same as our own.

The second danger in this situation is that its subjectivity will make it almost impossible to take into account changes in the industrial climate which will have a considerable impact on the business a few years downstream. This subjectivity encourages continuing the status quo, and the first thing we know we have a Cro-Magnon manager in charge of a 21st century enterprise. An executive, august though he may seem to his subordinates, is still a human being; he is subject to the same weaknesses and frailties as is the rest of mankind. Moreover, he often is not subject to close counseling in the matter of replacement selection. In fact, there may be a trend to keep the entire matter under a cloak of secrecy, with even his closest confidantes excluded totally from the process. This can mean that before there is general recognition of the personnel selected the die has been cast, with no possibility of early reconsideration.

It would be unfair to imply that all executive selection is made on such loose criteria. There are a number

of things which point to outstanding performance and
are indicative of untapped potential. Simple observation
shows outstanding performance on a basis of comparison
with the peer group. Consistently high performance evaluation by a succession of different supervisors is most
certainly significant. Another rule-of-thumb measure consistently applied is salary history. The basic fallacy here
is in not identifying and properly weighting the independent variables which may significantly affect a person's
salary progression.

Peer evaluation is never neglected by an alert executive. The trick is to elicit this judgment in a context
which will not make the meaning flagrantly apparent. Actually, it is not altogether impossible to get a peer assessment even if it is understood that a promotional evaluation is underway. Human nature being what it is, a
man is flattered to be asked his opinion of another by an
executive, no matter what the circumstances.

Most modern executives are now sophisticated about
the need for measuring a candidate's general developmental growth. There are recognizable milestone criteria
which can be applied on a time continuum with quite
clearly defined and valid comparisons.

Largely, our whole quarrel with all these methods
is their heavy dependence on intuitive and unsubstanti-
ated judgments. There must be a better method of equat-
ing individual differences and applying scientific methods
to the problem of executive selection.

There is another aspect to this picture which will be
looked at later: the possible reticence of the top executive
to face up to the problem of selecting his successor. This
has something of the timbre of picking out your casket
and your burial-plot. The greater any man's achievements
during his business career, the more natural it is that he
should dread the contemplation of its conclusion. Before,

when he passed the baton it was with the anticipation of going on to greater things; this time, his prospect is limited to hoarding his acquired resources, playing with his grandchildren, and the probable boredom concomitant with retirement.

The selection of executive replacements is of such critical importance to the continued success of any venture that it becomes imperative to put it on the most scientific and objective of bases. After all, no one is likely to be calm at the prospect of seeing his whole life's work vitiated as soon as he is gone.

NEED FOR RESEARCH AND PROGRAM DEVELOPMENT

The continual pressing need for the early identification of executive potential, plus the unscientific methods now in use for picking executives, shows an imperative need for a planned research and program development activity in this area. There is daily evidence that tomorrow's executive will no longer be able to bumble his way through with any possibility of success. The ever increasing complexity of our technology, the greater sophistication of our workforce, and the recent emergence of such disciplines as systems management, all militate against the future success of intuitive management.

A point in illustration is the vast change which has come over the business of government procurement during the past few years. Not many years ago, it was possible for major government contracts to be won on the basis of personal friendships or political influence. Hundreds of millions of dollars worth of federal contracts could be settled by personal negotiation between two people. This is no longer true. Department of Defense Directive 3200.9 spelled out quite clearly the general procedure by which all Defense Department procurement of weapons systems would thereafter be effected. This directive was then implemented with a number of manuals called "The 375-Series," which particularized the procedures step by step through such elements as the request for proposal, configuration management, systems management, vendor's management, and so on, right through the whole cycle. Another concept was included, after much debate, beginning with the C5A procurement contract, in which the competing vendors had to spell out in their proposal dollar figures for the entire weapons system, including even such things as necessary spares and training facilities. Proposals presented to the Defense Department by the two final bidders were likely to contain more than 6,000 pages and weigh a few pounds less than two tons when delivered in the required number of copies.

Hardly had the Department of Defense instituted this procedure than NASA and FAA indicated that they, too, would move in this direction. It is now clear that, in order to sell a major product to the government hereafter, a company will have to be prepared to go through this kind of procedural cycle. Another discipline included at present in government procurement is program evaluation and review technique (PERT), both time and cost. The PERT/time chart for a major weapons systems can easily extend for 70 or 80 feet around two or three walls of a control room.

These points simply reinforce the thesis that a modern executive must be sophisticated in such systems, to say nothing of other mathematical decision-making models such as operations research. We can only surmise what effects future generations of computers will have on the field of management.

The obvious answer to this challenging need will be interdisciplinary cooperation between the technologies involved and the behavioral scientists working as management development specialists. Basic research must be done to establish the minimal content of the new knowledge an executive will have to master, as well as the most viable training methods for accumulating this knowledge.

We must not conclude, of course, that all the new elements of an executive's development will necessarily be of so technical a nature. A vast amount of work remains to be done in the integration and delineation of the executive's place in a social climate which has undergone revolutionary changes within the past few years. It is also clear that this change is not yet completed. The inevitable conclusion of this chain of events is that the executive will be required to have much greater conceptualizing ability in the future than would suffice him today. In this context "the big picture" means a great deal more than simply an overview of his own company or one industry. The interlacing of any business into modern society is so tremendously complex that its conceptualization will be many times as difficult as it has been in the past.

It is not clear that a majority of our top business people yet realize the full implications of this matrix of change occupied by American industry. It is not even certain that a preponderance of our leading thinkers in the field of management have a sense of urgency about the tremendous task ahead of us. This is a simple fallout from a geometric increase in the complexity of our technology.

It is not enough to show the necessity for a vigorous program of research and program development for executive training; also implicit in this situation will be a concomitant duty of the management development specialists to conduct a hard selling campaign to top managers to convince them of the need for some fundamentally different and new approaches to executive development. It will be something like Louis Pasteur's campaign to sell the general public on the need for immunization against disease. Lack of familiarity with these new fields will be the smallpox of tomorrow's executive population.

As a result of the selling campaign maintained by the management development specialists, there must be developed a close working relationship between management development people and the key personnel in every function of the enterprise. These key people can make two critical contributions to the process. First, they can develop a fine sensitivity to the needs of their own management people and communicate these to the specialists. Second, they must also be prime resources for technical data to be included in new management training activities. The function of the management development specialist is to apply his expertise in the laws of learning to weld the technical data furnished by others into learnable units for those managers who have been determined to need this new material.

There is a secondary activity of management development people which should be ongoing—the training of trainers. It should *not* be the continuing function of the management development specialist to teach any program repetitively. Rather, he should teach pedagogical method to those line people who are willing to undertake a certain amount of teaching for their own personal development. This process of training the trainers is time consuming, but at least it does not restrict the management development personnel to only a few programs. Another desirable side effect comes from the involvement of line personnel in the teaching of management courses. This is the greater ego-involvement which usually occurs, with the result that the man who has been teaching will now be an active evangelist for the new cause, rather than just a passive believer.

The mechanics of course development by a trained specialist are not as involved and mysterious as many managers believe. The principal trick is to make good judgments concerning the amount of new material to be included in each segment of the training. This, of course, is closely related to the difficulty, or level of abstraction, of the new material to be learned. So far as some of the newer teaching techniques are concerned, the latest research tends to show little significant difference among them as to their efficiency. It therefore becomes largely a matter of choice on the part of the program developer, or the instructor to be used, as to whether new material might be presented as programmed learning, by the lecturette-discussion method, by the case method, by the Pigors incident process, or whatever other way might be thought of.

One or two good behavioral scientists can spread themselves over an amazing amount of a company's management in this area of educational research and program development. To reiterate, the war is basically won or lost in the selling campaign necessary to get management coming to the developmental specialist for help in this area.

If properly trained, the behavioral scientist will also be able to carry through in determining the validity and reliability of the testing instruments used. It will thus be possible to measure much more closely what learning has actually taken place as a result of the training. Management's major worry is that the proliferating technology will inundate the specialist with too many disciplines for him to follow through this process in an orderly fashion. There may be too many areas waiting for help simultaneously to keep all clients satisfied. The behavioral scientist

is rapidly becoming the fulcrum of the whole function of
management development.

REVIEW OF CONVENTIONAL METHODS OF EXECUTIVE SELECTION

There are several methods which singly, or in various
combinations, are used to identify executive material. As
has already been said, in the present state of the art none
of these methods is very scientific. However, when used
as objectively as possible and combined with the overall
judgment of those responsible for the selection, American business has done a passable job in the past as measured by the caliber and performance of incumbent executives. The catch is that these loose methods will not suffice in the changed situation we are now facing. We *must*
find a way of quantifying some of the elements necessary for the selection of executives. It takes precision instruments to do precision work. There will be about the
same similarity between yesterday's company president
and the chief executive of the future as there is between a
Model T Ford and today's Cadillac. Both have been very
functional, but in different surroundings. Perhaps we can
help ourselves to focus upon one of the most pressing
problems of American industry by checking off some of
the salient characteristics of our present selection methodology.

Performance review. As was noted previously, there
is a deplorable tendency for performance review to become extremely perfunctory during a man's years in middle management. Of course, his continued occupancy of
his position there is in a sense a continuous performance
review. But this still does not document the step-by-
step growth which is necessary as an indicator of still

further potential. When the man is being considered for elevation into the executive ranks, a careful examination should be made of his entire managerial career, beginning with the earliest records of his presupervisory selection. This is obviously another strong argument for the duty of his superiors to keep a clean-cut and definitive record of his progress in considerable detail. This is in no sense of the term any argument for a uniform method of performance analysis. Different levels, different climates, different functions, different supervision—all militate against there being a standardized form to which all reviews must be bent. What is essential is that there be a well-defined trail of reviews which constitute a tracking method.

Salary history. As has been previously noted, it is incontestable that a manager's salary history can be a significant indicator of his general potential. We have masses of statistical data which can give us normal salary progress for managers through any recent period of time. What must be kept in mind is that salary, like so many other variables, is a relative thing. Some of the factors which should be weighted when projecting a manager's salary curve include the industry itself, the function within the industry, the fiscal state of health of the companies which have employed the man, the numbers of managers in similar categories with which to compare him, and even such imponderables as the political strength of the manager's various supervisors. It would without a doubt be a Herculean task to attempt to reduce all these things to an actual formula that can be applied in evaluating a man's salary growth. But these factors must, in some way or another, be taken into consideration if salary history is to be used as one of the principal determinants in executive selection.

Peer evaluation. Survival in the managerial jungle can never be possible without continuous evaluation and re-evaluation of the competition. Consciously or subconsciously, day by day, peers keep track of peers. They are more keenly aware of strengths and weaknesses than are either supervisors or subordinates, because their own future is more closely tied to their peers' progress than to any other single factor. If a manager's peers can be made to talk candidly, their comments can give some expert advice concerning the promotability of any of their fellows. We shall have to leave it to the finesse of those responsible for executive selection to elicit peer evaluations which can be trusted.

Evaluation by subordinates. Those charged with the responsibility of picking new executives can never forget the importance of the subordinates' feelings about their supervisors. However, it is obvious that extracting a clear distillate which will be meaningful will be difficult when talking with these subordinates. They automatically build in too many safeguards when speaking about their bosses. Ordinarily, evaluation by subordinates must be compiled by indirection or even at second hand. This is a fine test of the sensitivity of the executive group in its day-to-day contacts with the lower echelons of management. However, every manager does surround himself with a reputation which grows by accretion from the bits and pieces of his interactions at work. A mosaic is formed, bit by bit, which, when analyzed properly, is as clear an identification as a set of fingerprints. The quaint old saying, "You can fool your boss frequently, but your subordinates never," has a real basis in fact. It is not even necessary to document subordinates' evaluation by chapter and verse, since the resultant entity, like the human body, is made up of innumerable single cells.

Management by results. It is heartening to note that a real ground swell is developing toward reliance on measurement by results attained by a given supervisor. Here, at last, we do have a method subject to a considerable amount of quantification. The process of cooperative establishment of goals and measurement against achievement of these goals is one of the least traumatic methods of managerial evaluation. Its objectivity removes most of the sting attendant upon other methods of evaluation.

Selection from outside. It is still common practice for a company to fill an executive slot by going outside. There is one strong argument for and one against this practice. Some maintain that to do so is an open admission of lack of general competency within the present organization. These are the people who are strongly committed to an unvarying policy of promotion from within. It is felt that bringing in a stranger acts so strongly as a demotivator on the present population that overall morale and productivity will be seriously endangered. This is quite probably true if there is a strong replacement for the executive vacancy. A man who has spent years preparing himself for a particular position, with full expectation of getting it, will be bitterly disappointed if he is passed over, especially for a stranger. He is correct in believing that his status in the hierarchy is threatened by such an event.

On the other hand, there are those who maintain that a judicious infusion of new managerial blood has a salutary effect on any organization. New methods, new approaches, and a fresh outlook on the organization can be expected to result in innovations which will be good. In addition, the proponents of this theory believe that an occasional stranger in the family will keep the old timers honest and hard working in their competitive activity. Again, it may be true in an enterprise which has been growing quickly that a vacuum will develop at the executive level because of simple lack of candidates sufficiently trained for positions at this level.

If this method is used, there are again two approaches to the recruitment of the outside talent. Company executives may make their own search, through their contacts in their own or other industries, and assume full responsibility for the quality of the recruit. This approach has the advantage that there will be repeated close contacts between the candidates and the company executives, so that relatively safe judgments can be made concerning how the prospect will fit in with the old organization as far as personal relationships are concerned. Or the decision may be made to use the services of one of the burgeoning numbers of "executive search" management consultants. These maintain up-to-date records on hundreds of executives and executive possibilities in many different industries. They ordinarily will have nothing to do with those men not already employed. First contacts are usually on a blind basis, with the prospect not knowing the identity of the company considering him. In this way, it is possible for the seeking company to have a good look at the qualities of many prospects without the embarrassment of having to turn down a number of candidates face to face.

It is true that there is a trend toward increasing mobility at the executive level from company to company. In many cases, this is the only way in which an executive can advance, either to a higher salary scale or to a bigger and more complex organization. As already noted, at this level a manager is in the business of management, and it actually makes little difference what the nature of the enterprise is. His executive functions are the same, no matter what company he represents.

Increasing span of control. It sometimes happens that none of these methods will expose a candidate who will satisfy those charged with the selection. A remedy for this situation may be the combination of functions under an existing executive, resulting of course in a broadening of this man's span of control. For example, at the executive level it may be decided to combine the manufacturing and engineering departments under one head, where before there were two executives reporting separately to the president. In one way of looking at this venture, some good results are possible. The executive charged with the new responsibility will broaden his perspective and gain new expertise. Also, the change will probably entail the appointment of two new assistants, with a corollary development of two new executive candidates.

There are many possible combinations and variations of the methods we have been exploring. Executive search always involves the attention and strong interest of the highest stratum of the company hierarchy. Ordinarily, it has sufficed in the past to depend on the good judgment of this group of men to come up with a competent candidate for the vacancy in the organization. In the future, this will be true in a rapidly decreasing percentage of cases. As has been insistently pointed out, we are faced with a major alteration of the whole industrial complex, with the result that old methods of executive selection will become obsolete within a very few years. The quicker this fact is faced by those concerned, the quicker we can get to work seriously on devising a better method of executive selection which will fit the complexity of the evolving industrial scene.

How Should It Be Done?

The choosing of executive replacements is of such importance to any enterprise that it must be done with care, precision, and forethought. First of all, it must be certain that the choice is in the proper hands. For reasons which will be explored more deeply later, it is debatable that the key executives of any company should have the deciding voice in the naming of their own replacements. Although it is true that in some companies the president is allowed autonomy in naming the man to succeed him, this is a questionable practice at best.

Most certainly, the board of directors should be deeply involved in this process, and it should have final say over accepting or rejecting the nominees for any post at the vice presidential level or higher. However, it is often a good practice to have a committee for the screening of eligible candidates, especially in larger companies, where there are many executives. This committee, usually composed of senior executives, can save much time and effort for the board of directors by eliminating the weaker candidates and leaving only a small field of well-qualified aspirants for the final selection process.

Second, a methodology should be evolved which is in consonance with overall company objectives and policies. The selection of different executives at different times on the basis of different criteria is inexcusable. It is all too easy for a brilliant, ambitious man to charm his way into the executive circle unless varied, objective criteria are applied rigidly whenever picking the new department head or vice president. It is here that a good, clean, well-kept development record can perform an invaluable service. If a man's progress from presupervisory selection all through his career in management is well-documented, comparison with similar records can be a much more exact instrument for selection. On examination, the kinds of difficulties he has met and his effectiveness in overcoming them will be fine predictors of his success at higher levels.

Management development specialists should be intimately associated with the whole field of executive selection. Their knowledge of management personnel, their association with the various candidates throughout their earlier developmental activities, and their greater objectivity because of their staff position make it imperative that they be deeply involved in this process.

Implicit in all of this, of course, is the matter of well-planned, long-term development toward this eventual goal. Executives should never "happen"; they must be grown in a proper climate by experts in the activity. The future health and survival of the entire business is deeply affected by this small group of key people; their choice should be most carefully made.

7

Executive Development

THERE is something of the same uncertainty as to the exact boundaries of executive land as there is in the case of middle management. However, the lack of sureness is not so gross as in the lower stratum. In the case of small or medium-size enterprises, it is relatively easy to determine which one, two, or three managers are the executives. In the large corporations, it becomes increasingly difficult to tell whether a department head is really a company executive or whether he is in upper-middle management.

WHAT IDENTIFIES AN EXECUTIVE?

Whether stated by company policy or not, there are some criteria which could be applied to determine which

147

manager is an executive. There will be some variations in these from company to company, but in the main they will be definitive in identifying an executive.

Amount and method of payment for services rendered. Although many middle managers get very respectable salaries (especially in engineering or other technical functions), there is ordinarily a relatively small gap between the middle manager's salary and that of his subordinates. At the executive level, on the other hand, there may be a spread of 200 or 300 percent between the pay of the subordinates and that of the executive. Seldom does anyone outside the executive group receive a cut of the incentive pay or bonus which is split among the executives in varying amounts, depending upon the current profitability of operations. The same is usually true of options to purchase stock at very favorable figures, now commonly offered as inducements to the executive group.

Scope of responsibility. In the thinking of some managers, a man is classified as an executive if he has total responsibility for an entire function. In other words, the director of engineering of a company would be an executive automatically in their thinking because engineering is one of the broad functions which in their aggregate comprise the organization. However, the responsibility for the function must be absolute. If there are various engineering groups with different reporting lines throughout the divisions of a company, the chiefs of the small engineering groups would not be given consideration as executives.

It is easy to visualize that the boss of one of the line functions would be considered an executive; it is not always as clear-cut that the manager of one of the staff functions is also at the executive level. This explains why it is only in the very recent past that most major companies have created a position of vice president of industrial relations. A few years ago, it was not uncommon to have the industrial relations function reporting to high middle management, well below the executive stratum. If an enterprise is properly organized, its staff functions will contribute just as importantly to the entire achievement of the company as will any of the line activities.

Policy-making authority. Any manager whose job description calls for him to make policy that is companywide in its effect is most assuredly at the executive level. The middle manager sets forth procedures to implement policy handed to him from above; the executive has the duty of supplying that policy within his sphere of control. This is not to say, of course, that he has unilateral authority to impose on other functions policy of his own design without first having coordinated it and received the blessings of his peer executives and of those to whom he reports.

Status. It has already been mentioned that executives customarily receive significantly higher pay than lower managers. In a sense, this sometimes approaches a matter of status rather than actual remuneration, our tax laws being what they are. But there are also many other status symbols which reinforce the position and dignity of the executive. In most cases, only executives are given company cars for their private use. The existence of an executive dining room emphasizes the separation of the executive group from the rest of management. Company-paid memberships in certain exclusive clubs are almost always reserved for executives.

In one company, an office went unoccupied for several months in a building where space was frantically being sought during an expansion program. The office remained empty because it was carpeted—only executives could have carpeting on their floors. In that same company, some of the bitterest political infighting was done by managers in the facilities department over the matter of square footage allotted to various offices; the prestige of position was significantly in proportion to size of office. In another company, no pictures were hung on the wall of any office except as they were issued from the office of the vice president of industrial relations. To the initiate, a casual glance at the pictures on the wall revealed immediately the position of the occupier of the office. It was not the pictures but the kind and cost of the picture framing which was the giveaway.

An objective look at these criteria should make it much easier to identify the executive group within any organization.

How His Job Differs from That of the Middle Manager

It would be an oversimplification to say that an executive's job is that of the middle manager, except broadened in scope and increased in depth. It is these things, all right, but it is more.

Part of the definition of an executive position is the matter of total responsibility for a group or a function. The executive has accountability to a much greater depth than do any of his subordinates. It is essential that such primary focus of responsibility be centered in one man if the enterprise is to succeed. The other half of this matter is that the executive is then charged with policy formulation for his area, while middle managers are not. The middle manager is an executor; his boss is the executive.

Another significant change occurring at the executive level is the sudden demand for sharply increased conceptual skills. The executive must be well aware of the present status of his industry and his company; he must also have a real sensitivity as to trends of future development for both his enterprise and the industry itself. His planning will be implemented several years downstream. If his organization is to continue to be successful, he must be right in almost every decision he makes. He does not have the same tolerance for error which he enjoyed during the years when he was in the lower echelons of management. His conceptualization of changes and growth in the organization will have an effect on everyone employed in the business. This means he must also be very much aware of the changes which will be necessary in company personnel if they are to fit gracefully into the company as he perceives it a few years later. His interest in and attention to the growth and development of his subordinates is very real and pressing.

Another facet to the life of the executive which will be strange to him at first is the much greater visibility to which he will be subjected. As a supervisor or a middle manager, he did enjoy a modicum of privacy which he will never have again. His every action will be examined critically by those about him. This includes not only those to whom he reports, but also his peers and his subordinates.

Closely allied with this internal scrutiny is his new importance to company public relations. As a recognized responsible executive for his company, he will be thrown into contact with a new set of associates in his outside business and social life. Even his casual comments will become newsworthy; he will no longer be allowed the luxury of freedom of opinion without first carefully assessing the possible effects of his remarks. Even such a professional executive as the president of a corporate giant found both himself and his company deeply embarrassed by a remark which he made in perfectly good faith and which he could have made without notice before he became the president of one of the biggest companies in the country.

Simply because of the position of the man who made the remark, a wave of unfavorable comment marred the company's public image for several years because of this trivial incident.

Most of the time, an executive's effect on public relations is limited to the community in which the business is located. But here, it can be of critical importance. If a business is so large that it exerts a dominating effect on the local economy, its executives will have to learn to live with being unpopular in the community. Their assessment of their public relations ability will have to be limited to keeping this public resentment from erupting into overt hostility. Politicians can be expected to attempt to gain office by campaigning actively against the "local octopus." They will also personalize their campaign by making direct attacks on the company executives. Since the newly elevated executive has been exposed to little of this in his former management career, he can easily panic and compound his difficulties in his public contacts. Another reaction sometimes met is to withdraw completely from the public scene and lose the battle by default. This is always a mistake.

Another difference in the executive's job from that of the middle manager is his much greater importance in his customer contacts. Since he will be working mostly with his opposite numbers in the customer companies, he may influence, for good or bad, the enterprise's entire business with any customer with whom he is in touch.

With a little good personal planning on his part, the executive will probably find fewer demands on his personal time. Those which do emerge, however, will be of much more importance than the ones he faced when he was lower in the hierarchy.

The new business life of the executive, then, will be significantly different from what it was when he was in the lower ranks. He will be given little time for a major read-justment in his own thinking and actions. This is irrespec-tive of how long he has had to prepare for his elevation to the executive rank. The change is almost as great as the one he made when he first became a supervisor.

Dangers of Increasing Isolation

It is not only the middle manager who lives in constant danger of becoming isolated from his people without even being aware of it. As quickly as the middle manager is promoted into the executive ranks, this danger is increased many fold. One of the most usual of the changed situ-ations is his physical location. As a middle manager, he normally has his office quite close to the function he heads. Executives, on the other hand, are usually grouped to-gether, and headquarters may be some distance from the firing line of actual company operations.

Elevation to a higher position in the organizational structure increases the percentage of time the manager spends in liaison and efforts of coordination. Executives' offices are together because a large proportion of their time at work is spent in each other's company. In fact, their subordinates will see less of them than will their peers. This further physical removal from the scene of the action, coupled with their interactions with others at their own level, makes it very difficult for executives to stay in touch with the "real world."

The day-to-day work of the executive is heavily asso-ciated with long-range planning and the development of any policy which will be a fallout of changes engendered by this planning. Our executive finds that he is more and more preoccupied with the conceptualization of the changes which will occur in his company as he reads the trends of the times. As he looks continually further and further ahead, it is quite natural for him to become much less preoccupied with the here and now. He trusts his lieutenants; he reads their reports, but probably finds it harder and harder to find the time for inspection trips through the work areas.

It will take his greatest power of concentration to maintain realistic touch with today's activities and, at the same time, spend so much of his time in contemplation of the future. In effect, it becomes easy for his big picture to get out of focus.

The best bet for the new executive who wants to avoid this kind of booby trap is to set up a simple control which will force him to make regular visits to the area of his responsibility. In addition to those things which he will see himself, he has a basic psychological factor working for him here. The natural tendency for subordinates to report to their boss only those things which they feel he will want to hear will be minimized if they know they can expect more-or-less regular visits from him. From his past performance and reputation, he is undoubtedly known as a man of keen perception and good analytical powers. He will be much harder to con into a state of euphoria if he maintains frequent contact with his area.

To complete the inspection of this facet of the executive's job, it should also be pointed out that a decent amount of isolation is not a bad thing for the man. He should have time for conceptualization and planning, for policy making and communication, without the countless distractions which otherwise would overwhelm him. He must have some protection against frivolous drains on his time, and a calculated amount of isolation will help to circumvent this threat. His secretary and administrative assistant can also be of immense help in this area, by assuming the responsibility of controlling access to the executive. It is true that we sometimes hear of the top executive who proclaims an "open door" policy and who announces himself as available to all comers. This type is rare and becoming rarer. One of the first adjustments the new executive has to make for himself is to discover the thin line of balance between desirable isolation and isolation that causes him to lose touch with reality.

Whose Job to "Develop" the Senior Executive?

If we hold fast to the thesis that the survival of any enterprise is dependent upon the continued growth and development of *all* its employees, then the senior executive must be included in this group. Actually, because of the critical importance of his influence on the organization it is of greater importance that a senior executive continue his developmental activity than it is, at the moment, for an individual lower in the hierarchy. In his position as guide and leader to other managers, the executive finds it mandatory that he be aware of trends in the business world—almost before they become trends; he must use his best powers of analysis and judgment to forcast the impact of a new management tool on his business; he must, in short, grow and adapt himself to a changing environment.

The basic rule has not been altered that the final responsibility for his development rests with himself. No one else can "develop" him any more than any other person can be developed by another. He must be constantly alert to areas affecting his job with which he has insufficient acquaintance. He must probe the results of his decision making for soft spots in his managerial expertise. He must be creative in searching out and making use of situations and techniques which will provide him with new learning experiences. The fact that he has arrived at the apex of the pyramid does not insure his remaining there. The smaller the area for footing, the more delicate is the balancing act required to maintain it.

And yet he has the same needs as does any other person for someone to whom he can turn for counsel and encouragement in this development process. Of course, even the president of the company has a boss—in his case, the board of directors of the corporation. He has every right to turn to this group for help in deciding what efforts will be most rewarding in abetting his growth. This can be done either in open sessions of board meetings or in one-to-one sessions with individual members of the board. For a proper perspective on his job, the top executive sometimes turns to those members of the board who are from outside the company. Their appraisal of his position and state of development can for this very reason be less biased than that of anyone who works for the same company.

Another source of counsel in the executive's development can be found among his business friends, such as an opposite number in another company. Appraisals of his state of development from such a source can be particularly enlightening and helpful.

Most certainly, there is another source of developmental help for the executive which must not be overlooked—the management development specialist. One of the things which gives the specialist an advantage over any of the other counseling sources is that he has an intimate knowledge of management at all levels in the company and thus is much better equipped to make comparative judgments about developmental levels than are some of the executive's peers, who have fewer and narrower contacts. It is really only quite recently that we see significant numbers of executives turning for personal counseling on their development programs to people within their own company. It should not be necessary to do more than point out the extremely sensitive and delicate nature of this relationship between executives and management development specialists. A spirit and demeanor of the highest sort of professionalism is the takeoff point for the management development man. Actually, as his contacts increase and he gains the full trust and confidence of the executive group, he becomes the repository of knowledge which is of vital importance to the corporate health and security.

Another demand is made on the specialist in this part of his job which can be nerve wracking. It is his duty to point out weaknesses and deficiencies in the executive just as much as in the first-line supervisor or any member of management at any level in between. The manner he uses in communicating his perceptions of the areas where growth and development are indicated is of fundamental importance to the success and career of the specialist, as well as having an impact on the increased efficiency of his company's managerial group.

In the long run, of course, every executive will decide for himself what counselors, if any, he will choose to help him determine and implement his developmental program. The fact that, in most modern companies, he does have a staff group with expertise in this area is an advantage to him. There can be no doubt of the increasing trend toward the judicious use of staff management development people in designing and building a more competent managerial group. Most corporation key executives no longer have to be sold on the idea that the survival of their company depends more on the quality of its management than on any other single factor. It is a small step from this concept to securing competent professional staff members to give assistance in this area. A very few years ago, staff people of this sort were considered to be vulnerable to the slightest dip in the profitability of the enterprise. They were among the first of the overhead to be jettisoned when the cash flow was reduced. It is probably significant of the increased recognition of the need for this kind of staff that in the past few years the picture has changed. Management development people no longer are considered so expendable at the first slight downtrend in a company's economy.

How Do You Make Generalists out of Specialists?

During the early history of American business, a majority of enterprises were entrepreneurial—they were one-man concerns. As this changed and the modern corporation evolved, we saw the emergence of the professional manager. However, because so many of the big new companies were based upon some sort of technology, a large percentage of top executives in these companies were men with technical or engineering backgrounds. Aside from these chief executives, most of the others had administration of financial matters as their point of entry into management.

It became noticeable to observers that these men had one common area of weakness: adeptness in and understanding of the human problems of management. Within the past few years, a trend has developed among college recruiters to have a look at the young graduates in the humanities and arts as possible managerial material for American business. This amounts to a tacit admission that we have underestimated the potential of the generalist as a manager. (The new president of Mills College, Robert Wert, in one of his first speeches as president, lamented the "desperate shortage of people who are truly generalists.") The man who has a good, broad education which touches upon many of the modern disciplines has a head start in the management field over one who is narrowly specialized in his education. At the managerial and executive level, necessary technical skills can be hired or learned quite quickly to the depth needed by the executive.

We do still have almost an entire generation of middle managers who will enter the executive field as specialists. This means that their efforts at personal development will be pointed toward changing their pyramid of learning into a sphere. They will have to graft more onto their area of familiarity than will a generalist, who is under the necessity of picking up quite a narrow body of new technical information.

Recently, as this problem has been recognized, many thousands of managers with technical backgrounds have gone back to earn an MBA degree, in the expectation that this will complete their broadening to a functional point. This device, however, still in the main omits any real exposure to knowledge of the behavioral sciences, the importance of which is growing at a more rapid rate than any other factor in the business life of an executive.

To reinforce this position, it should be reiterated that the most effective manager of the future will be the one who has basic familiarity with, and feels comfortable in, many disciplines rather than one. Another of the devices becoming popular to increase perspective among middle managers and executives is enrollment in "Great Books" courses at universities. Here, under the guidance of mature and widely read leaders, they can start to integrate concepts from many fields into their own thinking and can thus sharpen the quality of their decision making.

The point which should not be missed here is that the first step necessary to the transformation of a specialist into a generalist is the recognition of a felt need on the part of the man concerned. He must motivate himself to achieve this end in the shortest possible time.

So far as the implementation of this need is concerned, two of the commonest methods in current use have already been mentioned. These have been functional for many individual managers. If this need exists to sharpen the operation of a new executive, he should concentrate his best efforts on devising some sort of program which will be viable in completing this change in his approach. This is actually what we are after—a broadened perspective which will remove a strong tendency toward tunnel vision of any person who has spent too long in a specialty. For professional help in this activity, the executive should turn to his old friend, the management development specialist. Here once more the executive will be relying on the management development staff man's broad lateral and vertical familiarity with management and his seasoned judgment as to the relative importance of some of the gaps in the general educational development of the executive in question.

It is with this end in view that some companies are starting to use rotation of assignments even at the executive level. In some ways, this is easier to do at the executive level than in middle or lower management, since there will be less disruption of day-to-day operations of the functions involved.

Another consideration should be kept in mind constantly. It will be quite natural for the executive to do this sort of personal planning in increments of three, four, or five years. This is very laudable, but constant care should be taken to remain sensitive to major changes in the general body of management theory and knowledge. The sudden appearance of new concepts in managerial theory may necessitate major replanning in personal development programs at any given time.

HOW MUCH TRAINING AND DEVELOPMENT DOES THE EXECUTIVE NEED?

It is not at all uncommon for everyone, including the executive himself, to have a slightly patronizing air toward the term "training" as applied to the executive level. His status is such, and his previous accomplishments are so evident to everyone, that it is natural for people to wonder how much more training this man really needs. The fallacy in this reasoning lies in the fact that the new executive is now operating in a sphere which has some elements that are completely new to him. He has not before been under the necessity of conceptualizing the activity of his function as it will change with the economy and with technology. Neither has he before had nearly so much contact with opposite numbers on the outside. He must learn to relate his function, first within the framework of the industry, then with the economy at large.

There are some who state flatly that this sort of mental reorientation cannot be developed within an individual by means of what we ordinarily call training. It is their contention that either a person is naturally endowed with this ability or he will never have it. We have our increased knowledge of the behavioral sciences to thank for dispelling this myth. The transition from upper-middle management into the executive field is subject to just as much planning and organizing, just as much training, as is the change in any lower part of the managerial hierarchy.

What is significantly different about the executive situations is the very much smaller group of people who are in a position to give him any sort of counseling in this area. He is going to have to depend much more on his own powers of introspection and self-analysis to come up with an estimate of what remains to be done for himself in this new and critical part of his job.

We are all familiar with the good employee who is a failure as a supervisor because he finds it impossible to delegate properly. We have also seen excellent first-line supervisors fail when promoted because they found it too difficult to adjust their operation to the managing of managers. In exactly the same sort of way, many men who have been superb as middle managers flounder helplessly in the more rarefied atmosphere of the executive suite. When this happens, it is almost always from the failure to readjust mentally and deepen the perspective as required by the broader responsibility.

Conceptual skills *are* amenable to the training activity; no man should ever be written off as "untrainable" in this area. But it is most certainly true that there is a broad range of differences in the effort involved in making different individuals perceptive and comfortable in the executive work climate.

We must also remember how much a company's basic philosophy will affect the amount and kind of developmental work the new executive will require. If the company is strongly centralized, his planning will be of much shorter range and much more detailed than it has ever been before. He is going to have to plan for many more people now than he has been accustomed to. On the other hand, if the company is decentralized he is going to have to be prepared to pass the ball to subordinates who he feels are completely competent and totally trustworthy. He will have to be satisfied with much less detailed reporting through his office on a routine basis. This may involve a behavioral change on his part significant enough to require specific and in-depth training. Again, however, he is in most cases the only person capable of making this decision.

Although he is, almost for the first time in his managerial life, in a position where he could devote a considerable amount of his time to formal training, it is probable that the new executive will lean in the direction of devising some sort of on-the-job training to satisfy his felt needs. For one thing, he may hesitate to expose publicly the fact that he has training needs for fear of the possible reaction among his subordinates. He is aware that having their full faith and confidence is one of the most elemental of the requisites for his success in his new position. He may, therefore, make an effort to satisfy his training needs in a way less subject to public scrutiny than by going away to some formal training activity.

One thing is fairly certain. He is going to have to make some quick decisions as to the amount and kinds of training and development necessary to facilitate his growth into the new job, because he will have a relatively short time in which to demonstrate his capability to his new bosses. The adequate functioning of an executive is of such fundamental importance to the success of the enterprise that there can be little time allowed for readjustments and reorientation. The stop watch will be held on him by an assortment of people who are vitally concerned with his success or failure; he will have but one chance.

It is quite apparent that the executive must not allow this fact to throw him into a panic. If fear starts him running, it is a dead giveaway to his thinking; his judges will usually need no other evidence of his inadequacy in the new assignment.

What Kinds of Training and Development Are Needed?

Because it is becoming recognized that, in general, new executives have more need for training in conceptual skills than in any other area, the field of executive training has received intensive and concentrated attention from many agencies for several years past. The American Management Association and such schools as M.I.T., Harvard, and Stanford have well-structured and thoroughly researched courses in executive development. More recently, the institution of Sloan Fellowships at M.I.T. and Stanford provides a year's heavy work in a group composed entirely of executives. Competition among these class members is intense; the results of the stretching and competitive effort can be quite salutary on the executives undergoing the experience.

Another definite factor in the development of an executive is the contacts he makes more and more frequently with executives of other companies. These interactions can be productive of some of the most solid development the executive can make.

The rigorous scrutiny to which the executive is subjected by those around him because of the very nature of his eminence in the organizational hierarchy makes any deficiencies in his training visible. For example, if he has taken the financial management route for his climb to the top, he may be quite deficient in his knowledge of production problems, sales activity, or engineering needs. His first official contacts with the activities of the board of directors will reveal this to him in no uncertain terms. This kind of exposure to and acquisition of information is easily possible within his own organization and will be the more functional because it does bear directly on the business of his company. Once he has gathered the data pertinent to his operation, much good can be derived from a short seminar at AMA or a university in the theoretical parts of the function in question.

Another aspect of the desirable rounding out of the executive is made necessary by his continual acts of public relations in his new job. This is the time in his life when civic and community activities are indistinguishable from his work itself. In fact, they are an integral part of his job. Today's enlightened managers know that a corporation, as well as an individual, is judged on the quality of its citizenship. It becomes more common every day to see company chief executives in the thick of the fight for better schools, pollution abatement, and urban rehabilitation. They know that the success of their enterprise is inextricably bound to the existence of a sound and healthy surrounding. In an extension of this same concept, a noticeable trend toward executive involvement in practical politics is emerging. Where a few years ago businessmen either were disdainful of politics or ignored it altogether, they are now strongly urging interested employees to become actively involved in local, county, and even state political activity.

The essential leadership qualities of an executive also undergo quite a change with the assumption of the new duties. Whereas previously leadership requirements were limited to interactions with relatively few people, now the leader operates in a much broader, but less personal, context. In effect, he has had to become the symbol of a leader rather than a leader per se. This is not to say that leadership is less important in the executive position; instead, the activity is charismatic rather than strongly personal.

The architectural competence an executive shows in designing and building his own personal program of development will be one of the most critically important factors in his success or failure.

WHERE DO YOU GO FROM THE TOP?

One of the biggest and most persistent of the personal problems which may face an executive is that of continuing his motivation. When you have reached the top of the heap, what do you do for an encore? If there are no more really significant vertical goals to attain, how do you keep up interest in what might appear to be a static situation?

The answer is simple enough—job enrichment. If the executive does a competent job of self-analysis as he enters his new position, and if he follows through with a consistent and conscientious program of self-development, neither he nor the job he holds will be the same as he grows and matures. He will find major problems facing him whose existence he was unaware of before he broadened his own perspective. There will be new avenues of approach to some of the older problems. He will find himself increasingly concerned with the development of his subordinates; his own maturity will alter the standards by which he measures their performance.

Of course, his own self-actualization needs may cause him to do things the reasons for which are not immediately apparent to the uninitiated. For example, a second-line executive in a large corporation may "suddenly" decide to give up security, a large salary, and what seems to be a reasonable chance of eventually succeeding to the top spot in order to take the No. 1 position in a much smaller concern, where his salary will be smaller and his security will be totally dependent on his own efforts. The reason for such an action, if he verbalizes it, is usually "challenge." Like the mountain climber, he does it because it's there.

Again, once in a while we see a top executive in one business moving into the controlling position of a company in an entirely different industry. There have been some instances of outstandingly successful performance by men who have made this kind of shift.

Another way for an executive to maintain his own motivation is to set successively higher and higher goals for his enterprise in such things as sales, new products, profit margins, or general company growth. While fully cognizant that we are in a growth economy, he may set his own goal for his company's growth at so many times the national growth for the industry.

Some chief executives find their interest in research and development very much intensified shortly after their accession to the top spot. They realize that the thrill, excitement, and dangers of bringing out a new product will normally furnish all the incentive they need to keep their personal operation in high gear. Perhaps we could equate their challenge in this case to the drive which caused the pioneers to move restlessly on toward the strange and unknown.

For the man at the top, challenge also lies in the reverse of his situation when pioneering a new product. It devolves upon him in a very personal sort of way to keep his radar turned on 24 hours a day for the activities of the competition. He must calculate nicely what impact their activities and new products will have on the industry at large and on his company in particular. A true sensitivity in this area separates the industrial giant from the run-of-the-mill executive. An ability to forecast correctly the direction in which his segment of the economy will be moving in a decade is an invaluable weapon.

We come full circle back to a basic truism—any job

is what the holder makes of it. The moment the job ceases to evolve and grow, its holder has cause for alarm. This is an invariable sign that our executive has begun to stagnate and needs quick action to regain his perspective. His best recourse in this situation is to check thoroughly every trusted line of feedback that he has within the organization. This is the time when he needs most urgently a base of comparison between his thinking and that of his most trusted lieutenants.

Most certainly, this should be the richest and most rewarding period of the executive's business life. He should now gather the fruits of the years he spent in apprenticeship and be able to elicit the purest harmony from his industrial orchestra.

8

Phasing Out an Executive

$\mathcal{O}$UR young manager is no longer young. By a combination of skill, determination, hard work, and a little bit of luck, he has risen to a position of real eminence in the company hierarchy. He is admired, hated, loved, but above all else he is respected for the considerable contributions he has made to the success of the enterprise. If his career approximates the "normal" one of an industrial executive, there are several areas in which his personal contribution may be classified.

Productivity. If our executive rose through the ranks of the hourly employee, the odds are overwhelming that his personal productivity was significantly higher than that of his fellow workers. As he entered management, his crew was notable for its productivity; this was one of the criteria by which his repeated promotions were accomplished. This was not the result of chance. Our manager spent many hours of his regular work time and many hours of his personal time in calculating the methods by which he could raise his group's productivity above the average. At some time during the sequence, or more probably several times, he was an innovator. However, it is also highly probable that our comer never concentrated exclusively on production. He was well aware that this is only one facet of the concern of the good manager.

Quality. One factor which most certainly tempered his concern for productivity was the knowledge that poor quality, with its attendant rework, overtime, and schedule slippage, is a masterful thief of profitability. He knows that, in many cases, dependable high quality is a major determinant of repeat business and the best attraction a company has for satisfied customers. But, once more, he is conscious of the necessity for balance in his perspective and recognizes that he must not dwell on quality so excessively that other attributes are overlooked.

Profitability. The manager who is promoted never forgets one thing—in the final analysis, the definitive judgment of his value to the concern will depend heavily upon his contribution to black ink in the lower right-hand corner of the balance sheet. He feels a direct and personal responsibility to those who have invested their money in the enterprise; his fundamental charge is to return them a fair percentage on their money.

Personnel management. In becoming a successful executive, he has done his share, or perhaps a bit more, in leadership and interest in the growth and development of his human assets. This is irrespective of his interpersonal relationships. He knows that of the three M's— men, money, materials—men are by all odds the most important. He will never be any more successful than his people make him. He has both a selfish and an altruistic concern that his organization be a select and superior group. During the process of his own growth and maturation he has become more demanding of the people who work for him, but he has also been able to reward them more highly with promotion, prestige, and increased salary.

Leadership. There is more to executive leadership than the effect of the executive on those who report to him directly. He becomes a charismatic figure to many other people in the organization—indeed, probably to all employees. No person has ever succeeded in defining "leadership" adequately for everyone. Semantically, this term is at a very high level of abstraction. Yet, though few can verbalize satisfactorily about leadership, every individual responds instinctively to its presence in an executive. Somewhere along the line, our executive has become a leader. Moreover, by his precept and example he has inspired leadership among many who have worked for him, thereby multiplying his own effectiveness many times.

Structural design. Another contribution which any true executive makes to his enterprise is in the influence he has had upon the structure and form of the company itself. His conceptualization of company objectives and his work toward their realization has without doubt altered the structure he found when he entered the company. He has made a very personal and significant contribution to the overall success of the business concern for which he has worked.

ANOTHER MAJOR REORIENTATION

So, at the zenith of his career, the executive faces up to the fact that he is about to separate from his working life. He now becomes aware, if he works for the average company, that no one has given much thought to preparation of any company employee for retirement. He has grown from managerial infancy to a commanding, even awesome figure in the eyes of his peers. All this achievement stands to be suddenly and tragically vitiated unless he has been at least partially prepared for his traumatic separation from his career. It is true that in the more progressive business concerns there are some stirrings of an awareness of a problem here. Some companies have structured and functional systems of preparation for retirement of their senior citizens; as a whole, we are far from satisfactory performance in this area. We are statistically, but not personally, aware of what happens to the businessman who goes into retirement without preparation. He is a dead pigeon—quite literally dead within a tragically short time in too many cases.

Because of the single-mindedness and intense concentration with which the executive has met his job, he faces an even more severe reorientation at the time of retirement than does the "average" person. One of the reasons for this is that recreational activity has played a smaller part in his adult life than it does in the life of someone less deeply immersed in his occupational activity. Even though the executive may have taken up golf and bridge because he felt it was more or less required for his image as a businessman, in most cases he has not allowed himself to become as deeply involved with these pastimes as some others do.

One of the hardest blows the approach of retirement will give to an executive is the sudden realization of the loss of prestige and status which he will certainly undergo. No matter how much he may be encouraged to "come around and see us any time," he knows from his own experience in the past how insincere these invitations are likely to be. His own peers will be too busy to spend much time with him; the younger managers will regard him with poorly concealed amusement or pity. Where he has been used to having almost visible influence on the thinking of others in the enterprise, he knows that after retirement this influence will be dissipated immediately.

A second major and traumatic difference will be the disappearance of time pressure on his daily life. A man who was accustomed to living on a split-second schedule suddenly finds himself with nothing but time on his hands, and this can be frightening. Unless he has been carefully conditioned to this, he will discover that his panicky attempts to fill his days actually serve only to accentuate the emptiness of his life.

Again, no matter how competently and wisely he may have invested his savings, the sudden disappearance of a major portion of his income will be unsettling. It is probable that for a number of years he has seldom been bothered with worry about whether he could afford a given expenditure—now this thought is almost constantly with him. Moreover, his increased leisure brings up more frequent opportunities to spend, as he makes his effort to keep himself occupied.

The retired executive will find his social activity strangely upset. The same constraints and embarrassments which have kept him from returning to the business establishment will also be felt if he goes on seeing old friends on a social basis. This can be even harder on his wife than it is on him. The necessity of either curtailing his social activity almost completely or making a new set of friends will add to his discomfiture. Neither will he be attracted very strongly, at least at first, to the company of other retirees. The entire situation is too threatening to have it daily reinforced by the presence of other men in the same situation.

At about this time, he will discover to his chagrin that the members of his own family have grown away from him, are no longer in any real sense dependent upon him, and may even tend to resent any interference on his part with their established routines.

Any organized attempt at the prevention of this mental and emotional syndrome must be based on the premise that this mental set must be supplanted by a more positive outlook. It is in this area that forward-looking companies are concentrating their efforts at retirement training. The usual method is to encourage, over a period of several years before retirement, the development of hobbies. In fact, these should be of such kind as to compete actively for a significant part of the executive's time between his 60th and 65th year. On this premise, some establishments schedule a gradually reduced workweek until, during the last year before retirement, the executive is encouraged to be in his office no more than one or two days a week. If this method is used, it is self-evident that a capable replacement for the executive must be brought into tandem with him, to take up the increments of his job as they are dropped by the executive being phased out. This naturally poses some special problems to the understudy in tact and self-effacement.

Another way to ease the pain is to make of this five- or six-year period a time to increase public service and community activities. The executive will be welcomed eagerly by almost any civic or service group. He is still a functioning executive; his influence in the community is at its height. On the other side, the executive himself can truly feel that his activity in these services is making a real contribution to the welfare of the community. Or he might find it interesting to focus his activity on the political action of the community or state. Politics does not take the same discriminatory action against an aging citizen as does a business enterprise. It is entirely possible that our soon-to-be-retired executive can make a new life for himself in politics.

To reiterate, the important thing to keep in mind is that the executive must be prevented from thinking that his entire cosmos will be shattered by the arrival of his 65th birthday.

WHOSE JOB IS IT TO HELP?

If it has been established and accepted that the company owes it to the aging executive to help him prepare for retirement, who will then administer this duty? At first thought, this may seem to be the province of the management development specialist, for over the years there should have grown up between these two an easy working relationship with considerable depth of mutual understanding. The management development specialist has access to a wealth of material which can be helpful to anyone faced with imminent retirement. He also has much practice and considerable skill in the area of counseling. His empathy for the heightened emotionalism of the executive should be greater than that of many other fellow employees. Because of his intimate knowledge of the executive's growth and developmental pattern over the years, the specialist is in a much better position to suggest the kind of activities which will ease the separation process. In his position as counselor, he can also go the other way and work with the associates of the executive to see that they do nothing to increase the trauma of the man about to retire.

In spite of all these things which will make it possible for the management development specialist to render aid, there are two other people who can give greater help to the retiree in the long run. Those are his own boss and himself. The man to whom the executive reports has, of course, had a very special relationship with the executive. Although in some ways the superior-subordinate relationship may tend to be a little blurred and indistinct at high levels in the organization, in the final analysis its nature has not changed since our executive was an hourly employee. At this time, a little extra sensitivity on the part of the supervisor can do wonders in easing this transition. One of the best ways to bolster the retiree is to act in public as if there were no change coming. One of the more disturbing parts about being turned out to pasture is any visible indication on the part of associates that they are thinking of the event.

The second way in which the superior can be helpful is in keeping a close watch over the development of the executive's replacement and the gradual shifting of the workload onto his shoulders. Unless properly done, this can be openly disruptive and very painful to the retiree. One aspect of this which can be quite touchy is the matter of implementation of major change. Even though it is a change which the retiree might have been wholeheartedly in favor of, he will be disturbed lest this be a manifestation of the passing of control from him to his standby. His superior, by working closely with the person being eased into the job, can make this sort of thing much less painful to the man about to be retired.

Once more, the most important element of this whole situation is the man himself. Just as we have seen that any development which occurs is a product of his own action, so likewise his retirement will be more or less disturbing to him on the basis of his own attitude and frame of mind. At no other time in his life has the matter of emotional stability and mental health been of such critical importance. He has spent a lifetime under gradually increasing stress. His behavioral patterns have been structured about this stress as one of the more important facts of daily living. If he can maintain the same reactions to this greatest of all stresses as he has to the rest, he should weather the event without too much difficulty. He can look at his business career with no inconsiderable pride and satisfaction; the edifice which he has erected in the business world will be his own best monument.

RELUCTANCE TO TRAIN A REPLACEMENT

There are some senior executives, working under the childish but widespread fantasy that if you don't look at a problem it will go away, who refuse to train their designated replacement properly. Their desire to remain at the helm leads them to pretend that they can be irreplaceable if there is no one to take over from them. In a sense, they may be right. It is possible for a thriving small or medium-size business to be ruined completely by the departure of one key executive. For example, a young merchant started on borrowed capital in a store which he bought from the creditors of a bankrupt predecessor; by the sheer force of his drive and personality he made a huge success of his venture. He expanded until he owned a total of five stores in three cities. He managed to keep a personal touch in the running of all five stores. His store managers were made 40 percent partners in their stores. All were keen, sharp, and very active. But, with the death of the founder at age 47, each individual store lost a significant amount of its business. Instead of being notably successful, they barely stayed afloat.

It is understandable for a man who knows that he must go to be reluctant to share his hard-won expertise and accumulated experience with the person who will replace him. The symptoms of this condition are not difficult to spot. The executive becomes increasingly critical of his subordinate's performance. He may go so far as to question openly the other man's good judgment in major decisions. In some cases, a succession of assistants will pass through the office in a short time, owing to the executive's inability to find a satisfactory replacement trainee.

A certain amount of this distrust may also be shown to long-time friends and associates with whom he has worked for years. This paranoid tendency is perfectly obvious to the associates, and in some cases the result is an earlier retirement than was first planned. Self-discipline is the only way to forestall this. Better to leave a pleasant and admirable memory than to go out in the midst of discord and lost friendships.

Of course, it is always possible that the executive is correct in his assessment of the situation. There may be no replacement qualified and ready to step into his position. This can mean only one thing—less than adequate attention to management development in its most fundamental sense. If no functioning attempt has been made in the area of executive replacement, the entire organization may be found to be fatally ill. It may indeed be too late for corrective action in this sort of situation.

It is in this connection that the management development specialist can make his most valuable contribution to the enterprise's success. The long-term planning, the careful and delicate influencing of executive thinking, the planned and implemented executive development programs, the nurturing of more than one candidate for key positions—these are the tests of the specialist in this field. He must also be prepared to stand impregnable to the attacks of the prospective retiree. He may even lose completely the trust and confidence of the particular executive involved, but he will receive the support of other key people who can judge objectively what he is trying to accomplish.

Reluctance to enter wholeheartedly into the training of his own successor as his retirement approaches can also be a sign of undamped mental virility in the executive. He is still full to the brim with unrealized ambitions and plans for the company. He had hoped to accomplish so many things which he now suddenly realizes will not be done while he is in command. This is the rationale behind another device rapidly gaining usage by the more progressive firms. That is the matter of keeping the fully retired executive on the payroll in a consulting capacity. Actually, as he is freed from the pressures and exigencies of his regular business life, the retired executive may display a sudden wealth of new creativity and planning ability. Now, for the first time, he can make full use of his accumulated experience and put it to work in guiding the enterprise into the future. He will, moreover, experience to the fullest extent the satisfaction of his self-actualization needs. Bernard Baruch was hardly known as a national figure until he "retired" to a park bench as the unofficial adviser of several of our country's presidents.

This especially fierce resistance to an inevitable change is completely natural and predictable in a majority of cases; it should be met with a little extra understanding and tolerance. It will be one of the most visible symptoms of the stress the executive is undergoing. No person can be truly comfortable in the face of a major change in the position, habits, and activities which have been built up throughout an entire career. This man needs help.

Effect on organizational dynamics. The imminent approach of any company executive's retirement will upset the delicate balance of the upper and middle echelons in the hierarchy. The retiree's departure will leave a power vacuum of greater or lesser degree, depending upon his influence and strength within the organization. The forces which are unleashed by the retirement start to act well before the time of his actual leaving, and these forces act irrespective of the person named to succeed the man who is going. The resultant jockeying for position will intensify as retirement day approaches and may continue well beyond the departure date.

So far as the successor is concerned, little if any of his predecessor's personal influence can be passed to him. He must make his own way from scratch and stake out whatever territory he can by means of his own strength. This is true whether the replacement comes from within the existing structure or is brought in laterally or from the outside.

As in any other disturbance to a dynamic equilibrium, there are three possible results from a personnel change at the top. First, the change may be effectuated smoothly and with no visible disturbance of operational efficiency. Unfortunately, this result is quite rare.

The second possibility is that the upset caused by the power struggle can do serious damage to operating efficiency for a matter of weeks, months, or even years. In the extreme case, the organization may be completely wrecked. An internal struggle of any magnitude keeps other managers from devoting their full energies to their jobs as such. Decisions are delayed; significant trends may not be noted; the competition may seize this opportunity to pull away into a commanding lead. Key men, disgusted with the turn of events, may pull out and go elsewhere, leaving other serious breaches in the organizational structure.

It is an awareness of this possibility which reinforces the retiree's hesitance in naming his successor and devoting enough time to his indoctrination or training. The man about to leave mistakenly assumes that if he delays naming a backup he can prevent these events from occurring. On the contrary, the lack of any clearly designated heir apparent will insure their occurrence. When no successor is in evidence, the only things clearly certain are that the boss will leave and that somebody will assume his position of influence within the structure.

There is a third possibility: that the infusion of new blood, if strong and healthy, will actually result in a better and more functional structure. This occurrence is a product of two things: a smooth and well-handled induction of the new executive and the display of firm leadership on his part. Organizations, composed as they are of people, have many of the characteristics of families. As the patriarch indicates his intention to relinquish control, the other members of the clan assess the importance of this event to themselves in terms of their estimate of the strengths or weaknesses of the successor. If he immediately shows all indications of competency, there is a good chance that significant new progress will be made under his leadership.

At all levels of the executive's area, his retirement has its effect in changes in informal groups as well as in rearrangements of both their leadership and their effectiveness. To most informal groups, a change in formal leadership poses a threat of some magnitude, at least until they have assessed the new alignment. Any group threatened from the outside becomes much more cohesive. Its internal interactions are increased in number and in sharpness; its members will collectively display defensive behavior. Lateral interactions will also increase in number, just as the wagon-train scouts increased their alertness as they entered Indian country.

Because of uncertainty about the future, informal groups also will intensify their policing of the group norms during the transition periods. Deviant behavior on the part of members will be subject to much sharper punitive action on the part of the group. Old-timers may suddenly find themselves to be isolates in informal groups of years' duration, especially if they have failed in demonstrated sensitivity to the possibility of undesirable change.

Even if the retiring executive is aware of this chain of events, he will discover that he has lost much of his control over his people as he tries to lead them back into their old posture. This discovery in turn is bound to have an upsetting effect on the retiree. The obvious lessening of his influence over his people will be disturbing to him and will make more difficult his personal readjustment to his approaching departure.

To both the retiree and his subordinates, his severance poses a strong threat to their security needs. So long as this threat is apparent, social, ego, and self-actualization needs no longer exist; everyone is too absorbed in a more fundamental need to have any concern for the higher levels of needs.

Other members of management must of necessity be deeply concerned about the group dynamics of the affected organization during this time of change. Their ability to calm the waters will vary widely from person to person, but it is imperative that they do make a collective effort to give help and counsel to this part of the organization during the transition period. Of course, once in a while the situation is such that unavoidable upset is recognized and countenanced by the rest of management. If the retiree has "peaked out" several years ago and has been allowed to continue in his position out of regard for his previous contributions, everyone concerned realizes that quite fundamental changes will have to be effected with the accession of the new incumbent. In other words, there must be some sort of therapy for the sick part of the organization, and its imposition may be unpleasant to all concerned.

The replacement may be the wrong person. It is entirely possible for the designated replacement to be completely wrong for the spot. This can happen especially when the retiree has become so engrossed in introspection concerning his own leaving that he is out of touch with the industry at large and misjudges his own company's present status.

Say, for example, that the incumbent was a financial man and had made his unique contribution to the enterprise because of his ability to watch over and guide its financial progress. During the years he has succeeded in solidifying the company's financial position into one of impregnable strength. In the meantime, the general economy has undergone significant and major changes which he has failed to evaluate properly. This was the situation with one major corporation immediately after World War II, when its management sat on a cash surplus of hundreds of millions of dollars, waiting for the postwar recession which never came. While it was in this state of hibernation, its principal competitor left it far behind, and the corporation has never regained its position of parity with its competition.

Another much smaller company went through a similar type of struggle with even more disastrous results. Its founder was an excellent entrepreneur; he exhibited great personal charm and leadership, and he had the deepest devotion of his subordinates. The selling organization was alert and hard-hitting; the customers were satisfied and loyal. The fatal flaw was that the owner failed to evaluate properly and respond to technological changes which occurred in his industry. Because he persisted in being satisfied with the status quo, he was outdistanced by two of his principal competitors; and, when he came to the time of life when he wanted to retire and pass the business to his son, it was discovered that in effect there was not much of a business to pass on. The final decision was to liquidate.

One lesson that can be drawn from this is that the natural tendency to look for a successor much like the incumbent is sometimes a dangerous thing. Perhaps the climate is now such that a different type of person should be put in charge, with a completely new methodology and approach to the operation of the business.

This matter of succession to a major executive's post is of such critical importance to the business that it strongly suggests the choice should be made by people other than the incumbent. The custom of allowing the retiree nearly complete autonomy in naming his successor is a fine personal gesture if the enterprise is sure it can afford to live with the consequences. The ego-involvement of the retiring executive is too great for him to maintain the necessary objectivity in making his choice. In demanding certain characteristics in his replacement, he may be practically assuring a tragic outcome by reinforcing things detrimental to the organization.

There is another aspect in picking a "look-alike" as a successor which should be carefully evaluated. The fact that the new man is quite similar to the old boss may actually work against him because of the constant reminder of the ways in which he *differs* from the "old man," thereby making impossible a comfortable readjustment on the part of the other members of the working group. Maybe it would be better to have a new leader so dissimilar that there would be a quick and complete erasure of the memory of the one just gone. This is why the younger brother or the son of a popular public figure may have an especially hard time winning popular support in his own right.

The change that occurs in an organization when an executive retires is much more than a changing of the guard. There is nothing routine about the event. The rest of the employees are psychologically and emotionally keyed to a high pitch; the effect of the new leadership now grafted onto the organization is much deeper than the effect would be if the incumbent had changed his managerial style or method of operation. Because of this hypersensitivity of the personnel at the time of change, the man being brought in or promoted could be the wrong one here, even though he would have been the right one in other circumstances. It is for this reason that intensive scrutiny of all these independent variables must be given by those responsible for naming a successor to the retiree. In the same line of reasoning, those responsible must also devote more time and care to supervising the indoctrination and "settling in" period of the new executive. Now is the time for frequent—even continuous—checks and rechecks on the morale, productivity, and general attitude of the people responsible to the new boss.

This is the time to get one true measure of the essential character of this part of the organization. The reception of and response to the new boss will determine his ultimate success or failure within a very short time.

THE AGING EXECUTIVE MAY HOLD THE ORGANIZATION BACK

One of the natural concomitants of advancing years is an increasing conservatism and a slackening in general effectivity. As an executive approaches retirement age, he may become reactionary without even recognizing it. His influence, both formal and informal, upon his organization will naturally tend to reflect the changes in his own thinking. One of the first symptoms of mental aging is a reluctance to make major decisions. This is especially true if the implementation of these decisions would involve basic changes in philosophy or operations in his area. Whether he realizes it or not, the elder executive becomes increasingly intent on maintaining the status quo, since it has represented successful achievement. Moreover, there is a strong tendency on the part of the average employee to imitate the style of the leader. If he has become conservative, their movements toward innovation and creativity will be inhibited.

This process of losing the momentum necessary to maintain leadership can be so slow as to be unrecognizable by the people involved. Many times, the only way this will be discovered is by comparing this part of the organization with others which are under younger and more vigorous leadership. If the executive in question is president of the company and therefore casts his shadow over the entire enterprise, such comparisons would have to be made with "opposite number" organizations in the industry. This kind of frequent pulse taking is one of the most significant contributions which can be made to any organization by its management development specialists, under the research and evaluative section of their franchise. One of their continuing activities should be a running comparison of their company's position with reference to the competition in the rest of the industry. Their assessment will not, of course, be final, but their reports to top management should receive careful consideration when their reading shows a loss in competitive position or a failure to keep up with an advancing technology. This watchdog function is shared with others such as market research and finance, but it must be done out of sheer self-protection if the company is to remain healthy.

There is more to this than just a comparison with others. If the influence of an older executive is slowing down his entire group, very probably the group's productivity and general efficiency will deteriorate from its own standards. That this condition is a subarea of the management field itself has been recognized by Professor John B. Miner of the University of Oregon. His book *The Management of Ineffective Performance* * is a classic. The handling of either production workers or managers who are capable of extremely good performance, but are not giving it, presents one of the more difficult problems to any executive. This is especially true when the situation arises, as described here, from the leadership of the group itself.

Where the executive's influence on his group is known to be the cause of deteriorating efficiency and productivity, this must be the signal for immediate action on the part of the rest of the executive group. If personal counseling with the prospective retiree does not bring him back into line, there will be little choice but to advance his retirement date and make possible the reclamation of the work group by the induction of a new leader.

Mandatory Retirement?

This chapter has been describing at some length the feelings and reactions of a man who is faced with mandatory retirement from his business affiliations when he reaches age 65. This has been done because an overwhelming majority of American businesses do have strict policy setting the time at which an employee must be retired. The reasoning for this posture is logical. First of all, if an executive remains at the helm for an indefinite

* John B. Miner, *The Management of Ineffective Performance,* McGraw-Hill Book Company, New York, 1963.

period he may gradually cease to be effective in his operation, with resultant harm to the whole enterprise. Second, his staying in power will strongly demotivate the younger executives below him, who will be able to see no clear line of progression. It is this latter fact which weighs more heavily in the rationale for retirement policy. The men at the various higher management levels in the larger companies know to the month the succession of movements which will give them a chance for at least a few years in the top spot.

Those who argue against a policy of mandatory retirement at a fixed age do so in the firm belief that mental health and creativity are not necessarily correlated on a one-to-one basis with chronological age. We have too many historical reminders that some of the greatest contributions to the welfare of others have come from men in their seventies or eighties. The major point to the argument against mandatory retirement is that the prospect of being forced into retirement at some arbitrary time will have a damping effect on any man's creativity. Why should he work for and implement some of his greater contributions when he knows that he will not be around to see the rewards come in?

There is another viewpoint on the matter of retirement age which deserves a good look before it is voted down; that is, an annual evaluation should be made of key executives' physical health, mental health, stamina, and ability to carry on business as usual. If there is no significant decline in the man's performance, why should he be discriminated against because of the clock? These evaluations should always be conducted by personnel who have no other involvement with the company, so that their integrity and lack of bias will be perfectly apparent. Any doctors, psychologists, or other specialists called in to make such a value judgment should certainly be in a position where they can both claim and practice the highest kind of objectivity.

No matter what a company's philosophy may be in this area, the country is eyeball to eyeball with one situation that cannot be ignored. The low birthrate in the 1930's is creating dangerous gaps in what will be the middle management and lower executive areas within the next few years. Working to aggravate this situation is, of course, the growth and increasing complexity of our modern corporate hierarchies. As this becomes more and more of a problem, there will be only two alternatives: Promote young men into higher echelons before they are ready, thereby geometrically increasing their chance of failure, with resultant harm to the company; or ask that the older executives remain at their jobs for a longer time. Of these two choices, the latter is much more attractive and less of a risk. As a case in point, a young man of 34 was promoted three steps in one movement— from the managership of a small service department to the general managership of the entire plant. His failure to rise to his new responsibility had a serious effect on his health and on his domestic life as well as on the plant itself. He was saved by transferring him to the No. 2 spot in another plant and giving him more time to grow before his next promotion.

By keeping an older executive in charge beyond his normal retirement age, advantage may be taken of his accumulated expertise without risking a failure such as was just described. Moreover, on a planned basis, this time may be used for intensive training of the replacement designee. His induction into the new job can be at a pace leisurely enough to remove much of the upset he will feel when thrust suddenly into the top spot. Again, under this procedure, judicious use can be made of the gradually shortened workweek of the older man, until he is at last phased out completely.

This is another illustration of a basic truth. No policy is sacrosanct if there are fundamental changes in the situation. The company which remains flexible and maintains continuous surveillance of its policy is the one which comes out ahead over the long haul, if it makes the obvious and necessary changes from time to time. The ongoing virility and strength of the enterprise are closely associated with the manner in which management handles the retirement of its aging employees.

9

Methodology

$\mathcal{W}$E HAVE followed the progress of our typical manager from the time someone other than himself thought he had managerial potential, through his long and busy career as manager, and on to the point of retirement. In discussing the ways in which he developed to meet his broader authority and heavier responsibility as he rose in the company hierarchy, many techniques have been mentioned which may be used in this developmental process. However, no methodology has yet been collected and arranged in the logical (and chronological) way it will have to be used if it is to be effective. At least three people should be involved in considering, evaluating, and selecting the different methods and procedures for effecting our manager's development: the manager himself, the manager's superior, and the management development specialist. Their interactions and cooperation must become flawless if we are to do the right kind of job. The one thing all concerned must learn early in the game is that management development is not a some-time thing. The attitude toward and thought about the development process must be a continuous activity. Frequent value judgments must be made, and the rate of development is directly proportional to the kinds of developmental activity which are chosen.

THE APPRAISAL PROCESS

The key to any successful developmental activity is the appraisal process by which the man measures himself and is measured by his superior or superiors. Day-to-day coaching by the superior will never do this part of the job by itself. At some stated interval in time there must be an objective effort at a formal measuring procedure. The basic reason for this approach is to get a proper balance between strengths and weaknesses. The average superior, in his informal coaching on the job, is managing by exception. Unfortunately, he is prone to notice and remark on only the negative exceptions. He may, of course, comment in passing on a job exceptionally well done, but the tendency is to dwell on mistakes made and ways in which to avoid repetition of these situations. An annual or semiannual casting up of accounts, which will force the entry on both the debit and credit sides, is a much fairer and more functional approach to the appraisal of a man's performance.

The second reason for keeping a record of our manager's progress will become apparent later as we look into the management inventory in more detail. It should be quite clear, however, that no complete inventory can be achieved by guesswork in a company of any size. There

has to be adequate documentation of the human components which make up the inventory, at least with respect
to their performance over the years.

The performance appraisal is also one of the major
elements going into the data bank for personnel research. This activity is of rapidly increasing importance
to the management development specialist, but its usefulness will be dependent on the amount and validity of the
data available to him. Similarly, any efficient determination of management training needs can be made only
from a solid basis of performance appraisals.

Many companies, governmental agencies, and other
employers of large numbers of managers have now involved themselves in some sort of routine and repetitive
performance appraisal. Two points should be underscored
as ways in which to progress and become more functional
in this activity. The first is to be sure that, insofar as is
possible, every element of subjectivity has been removed
from the measuring criteria. Both subordinate and superior will have a basic distrust for the viability of any
method of appraisal based on value judgments of traits
or characteristics. The sad fact is that it is easy to dream
up an appraisal form which has a specious appearance
of validity but which, on closer analysis, is found to be
purely subjective in nature. This sort of system will
invariably bog down and come to a halt in the second or
third round of its use. Although a manager may recognize without much enjoyment that he sometimes must
cast himself in the role of judge, he will totally rebel
against a situation which calls for him to be judge, jury,
and executioner. If he doesn't, his surbordinate will.

The second item of change to be strongly urged on
most companies in their appraisal system is the personal
involvement of the appraisee throughout the entire
process. It is highly unnerving for a manager to discover

suddenly that he has been the object—we could almost say the victim—of a formalized measuring procedure of which he was totally unaware. The mental set and bias evoked by this procedure will make it impossible for him to derive any real good from the process. On the other hand, if he is personally involved from its inception to its conclusion, he will be much more likely to believe in its essential fairness and will be predisposed to gain what is intended from any objective performance appraisal. At the same time, the superior will also have a better attitude toward the activity as he sees and recognizes his surbordinate's contributions to his own performance review.

The position description. The sequencing of the appraisal process is logical and invariable. The first step is to set the limits within which the manager's job will be confined, and it should be remembered that this will be static for never more than a few months. Therefore, the position description must be rewritten every time a performance appraisal is conducted.

It is essential that both the manager and his superior write a position description for the manager. It must be done independently, so that neither will have a twisting effect on the other's view of the job. It is enlightening to see how far apart the ideas of the two men may be concerning the manager's area of responsibility. If there is a large difference between the two concepts, the two viewpoints *must* be reconciled before going any further in the appraisal process.

It is this honest misunderstanding of how the other sees the position in question that causes many of the basic troubles between superior and subordinate on the job. For example, if the subordinate is more than usually aggressive, he may see his sphere of authority as much larger than his superior will think has been indicated. Then, when the subordinate apparently far exceeds his stated authority, the boss will become irritated and question the judgment of the subordinate. The latter will be disgruntled at what he may consider to be "delegation on a string." If consonance is reached in the thinking of the two men about the job, a much more harmonious work climate will be possible.

If the manager demonstrates a significant and reasonable amount of growth and development from one appraisal period to the other, his position description must be rewritten because his job must be made to expand to his new and greater performance capability. Again, however, there must be a reconciliation between the thinking of the subordinate and his superior.

There can be a wide latitude in the format for writing a position description for appraisal purposes. Certainly, it will not have to be in the cramped and stylized usage of wage and salary people. There are many subtle facets of a job which can be pinpointed in the appraisal description, but which would be completely useless in terms of job evaluation for wage and salary people.

It might be well to consider at this point a curious attitude exhibited by a great many companies that follow a formalized management development procedure. They make a strong point of the fact that performance appraisal for management development purposes should never be used for salary review. This position is completely irrational. When the development appraisal is done honestly and without bias, there is no reason in the world why it cannot be used as the basis for the annual salary review. Should it not be used in this manner, there can be only one question in the mind of the manager— which of the two appraisals is then going to be a dishonest one? If the standards determined for measurement of his performance for appraisal purposes are honest, they should be perfectly functional for assessing his merit rating position. In fact, the most pragmatic approach is to have the development appraisal process geared to coincide with the merit rating procedure.

There is another specific organizational advantage to be derived from this repeated look at the positions of all managers. It can be used as a control against a fair and equitable distribution of labor among the management members of the organization. What actually happens is that this process gives continuing visibility to rates of growth among the different managers. It may even serve to indicate when one man is overdue for promotion because of an exceptional rate of growth. Most of the larger companies have wage and salary structures allowing for a "bracket" upgrade within the same titular position.

Here at the very beginning of the appraisal cycle is also the proper place to start serious and complete record keeping. Because of the sensitive nature of the information elicited during the formal developmental cycle, many managers hesitate to institute and keep up formal records of the proceedings. This is again illogical, since these same managers would be horrified at the thought of incomplete information in the company records—or a lack of records—concerning salary matters for the same subordinates. It is true that proper security measures must be strictly maintained throughout the entire process. In many cases, separate files for developmental purposes are kept for all managers and are not filed with their regular personnel jackets. If it is felt desirable, the typing of all appraisal papers may be given to one secretary whose discretion is beyond question.

Since the balance of the entire appraisal process rests on the fulcrum of the position description, it follows that it is hardly possible to give too much care and attention to it. In some instances, it may take a longer time to derive a document acceptable to both the manager and his boss than to do all the other formal paperwork involved with the appraisal. The description is the standard of standards for the whole activity; its final form will govern the attitude toward and value received from the rest of the appraisal. That the exact format for this type of document cannot be shown on a universal basis should be obvious. The simplest form which is functional in the eyes of any organization's management should be used, and it should be easy to introduce changes in the accepted format whenever they appear to be useful.

Setting the goals. To many managers, the process of goal setting holds all the distrust of the unknown. Unless they have been accustomed to a results management approach to their work, they think this process is either useless or too esoteric to be of any help on the day-to-day job. In this area the management development specialist can be of real value to the manager by explaining the process and working through with him the first set of goals in his new development program. Psychologically, the best time to introduce this concept is when the manager first becomes disturbed at trying to work with an appraisal done in subjective terms.

Once more, the manager and his boss should develop goals for the manager separately, then reconcile them in a face-to-face meeting. Normally, when the manager first undertakes to set his own goals, he will have a tendency to set them unrealistically high. Then, when his failure to achieve them is quite spectacular, his reaction will be a distaste for the whole process. The second common mistake is to include too many individual targets during a single measurement period. It is far better to have three or at the most four major goals for a six-month or one-year period than to try to fractionate the manager's effort among ten or a dozen separate projects.

Customarily, there is a tendency to concentrate on setting goals for improvement in the areas of the manager's weaknesses. In the interests of developing a well-rounded manager, this is quite defensible. The manager will have an unconscious tendency to turn to his own strengths in his daily operation; unless he formally maps a campaign, he will also have a tendency to ignore or avoid his areas of weakness. His greatest promise of development will come from this forced attention to the latter.

Of greatest importance is the matter of setting goals in terms that are directly quantifiable. This presents no problem to the line manager. It is relatively simple for him to set goals in percentages of increased production, decreased costs, or decreased rejects and attendant rework. To the man in the staff position, it usually presents a real problem in conceptualization to establish goals in his service function which are directly measurable. But it can be done. Especial care must be taken by the staff man to be sure he is setting quantifiable goals that have real significance. We can look, for example, at the typical training section in almost any American industry. There, reporting will normally be done in terms of man-hours of instruction, either paid time or off hours. This, of course, is significant to an extent, but of far greater importance are the behavioral changes which come about as a result of the instruction. This may be more difficult to measure; but it is possible, with care and well-designed instruments, for the behavioral scientist to come up with a close approximation of whatever changes have been effected. This is just another way of reinforcing the fact that the quality of a staff man's work is at least as important as that of the line production man. The same standards of quantity, quality, and costs should be applied to the work of the staff man as are used in appraising the work of the line manager.

It should already be clear that a considerable amount of planning will have to go into the establishment of these semiannual or annual developmental goals. The best possible use should be made of historical data, and the accumulation of pertinent facts now takes on a new significance. The manager's judgment will have to be sharpened in determining which of the data manufactured in normal operation are significant and should therefore be preserved in an easily retrievable form. As this habit is established and reinforced over several appraisal periods, the development of the next goals will seem to be much simpler, although actually more work will have gone into their formalization.

By using goals of this sort, a much more meaningful pattern of communication will be established between superior and subordinate. In tying the actual operations of the function to the developmental goals of the manager in question, the most economical and pragmatic methods of operation will certainly emerge from the process.

There is, of course, one corollary to this which becomes evident. No developmental goals should be "set in concrete" any more than should any other type of objective for that part of the organization. It is perfectly possible for conditions over which the manager has no control to change so radically that the goals he had established for a given period would become totally unrealistic. He must be as ready in this matter to make necessary changes and adjustments as he is in any other part of his operation. The accomplishment of a set of realistic goals (which yet are high enough to make the manager stretch) will do more to instill self-confidence and will give more of a sense of real achievement than anything else the manager can do in his day's work. This is the real measure of manager development.

Measuring achievement. Measuring results against a good set of already established goals is one of the easier parts of the appraisal process. The yardstick is there; the subject is put beside the yardstick; the growth is measured. The problem emerges if performance has been too much greater than the goals or if it is too far under what both the manager and his superior agreed was fair for the appraisal period.

In the process of examining the reasons for over-performance or underperformance, real learning can take place. It is understood that neither the manager nor his boss will rationalize away variances from the goals, but will search for and come up with the real reasons for this difference in results.

If, for several appraisal periods, the manager has consistently performed significantly above the established goals, it simply means that he has not been stretched enough by the norms set up. This is easy to correct. On the other hand, consistent underachievement of realistic goals is a signal for some pretty thorough and penetrating self-analysis on the part of the manager. The results of this activity should then be checked with his superior and the management development specialist for their corroboration or change. In this situation a complete look should always be taken at performance in the five basic functions of the manager. Perhaps his failure to achieve his developmental goals is associated with poor general planning. Or it may be that he has been lax in setting up a workable set of controls to pace himself through the appraisal period. In many cases, because of interpersonal problems resulting from poor direction, he has failed to establish his leadership over his men, and they either have not seen the challenge or have failed to rise to it.

This type of analytical work coming as a result of failure to meet developmental goals will have a fallout of suggested corrective methodology. It is another time to enlist the professional services of the management development specialist and call upon his knowledge of and experience with corrective methods for these basic lacks. (It is easy to see at this point that a couple of steps in the appraisal process—the interview and developmental planning—have been omitted. These will be considered later; it is the intent here to show cause and effect between failure to meet standards and the determination of a viable solution to this problem.)

We should remember that underachievement of goals is not *always* the result of a failure or weakness in the manager. Unforeseen forces may have changed the situation to such an extent that it simply would not have been possible for the manager to reach his goals for the appraisal period. A major breakdown of equipment, labor troubles, difficulties with vendors, an unanticipated serious recession in the industry at large, or a combination of these and other factors over which he has no control could adversely affect the manager's performance against his goals. However, these are usually so visible in retrospect that the manager would never be unjustly penalized for this kind of situation. But the manager who is clearly a comer and noticeably better than his peers will undoubtedly have planned for some of these contingencies in establishing his developmental goals.

It is quite usual for the working relationship between the manager and his superior to undergo a major change after a few rounds of the performance appraisal. Any tendencies to a relationship of dependency on the part of the subordinate will by this time have been replaced by an atmosphere of much closer cooperation, but with more decisive action on the part of the manager. That is to say, he will show signs of maturing within his position and in his managerial relationships. There should also be evidence of stronger leadership shown to his subordinates, as well as improved morale among his people as they see signs of solid achievement based on adequate planning.

If our manager is normally intelligent, there should be another plus from his continued attention to his own developmental cycle. His personal reaction to a more participative management will probably make him want to extend the experience to those who report to him. He can get extremely valuable help from his people by involving them in the formulation of his own goals, since they will unavoidably be closely associated with his achievement or failure. In the ultimate extension of this concept the manager will find himself operating most of the time in the 9-9 managerial style.

There is one last consideration in the measurement of results against established goals. It is of critical importance that the measurement be done promptly at the close of the appraisal period. As our manager becomes more deeply involved in this cycle of developmental activity, he will realize that there must be no hiatus from the close of one cycle to the beginning of the next. Although the appraisal periods are time-limited they should be considered not as discrete units, but as mileposts on a time continuum. To recapitulate, whether the measurement shows results to be under, on, or above goals, our manager at least knows that he is being judged against honest and fair norms.

The interview. The key to the entire appraisal process is the interview between the manager and his boss after the measurement has been completed at the close of the appraisal period. Both men already know in their own minds what has been accomplished during the period, as well as the areas in which the manager failed to reach his goals. Nevertheless, the verbal interaction between the two men will make the entire process seem official, particularly to the manager.

Many things have already been written about the importance of notification, surroundings, the climate established by the superior, the maintenance of a truly objective attitude, and allowance for as much discussion as the manager feels is needed. In spite of the voluminous literature, it is important to the continuity of this treatment of the process to recall once more the place of all these items.

The appraisal interview should have a status with both the manager and his superior which would demand that a formal notification be given to the interviewee of the time established. Sufficient lead time should be given to allow thorough preparation by both parties, yet it is important that the interview be held soon after the measurement has been completed, so that developmental planning can be done and the cycle can begin again with as little interruption as possible.

The setting should be worthy of the seriousness of the occasion. Many managers find it worthwhile to hold the interview somewhere other than in the normal work surroundings. It is felt that it will be easier to achieve good rapport, as well as more complete communication, if the interview is held on "neutral ground." There should be no need to dwell on the necessity for a quiet, undisturbed situation.

A good basis has already been provided which will make it easy for the superior to set a climate which is apparently quite permissive, yet which is in actuality subtly directive. The manager knows exactly what he wants to achieve during this interview, but he will probably not know specifically the route to his objectives until the actual interview takes place. The crux of this whole matter is the attitude displayed by the superior and the way in which he directs the interview without giving the appearance of leading it in any specific direction.

If these prerequisites have been observed, the maintenance of objectivity by both parties will be easy. Of course, this objectivity will be erected on the foundation of the goals which were agreed upon at the start of the appraisal period. The framework is already there; it takes little effort to continue without the interjection of personalities, with all of the emotion that this immediately evokes. When the manager has disciplined himself in such a way, it is usually a relatively simple matter for him to recognize his own weaknesses and to see and accept the value of the suggested remedies.

It is never possible to predict with any accuracy the length of time it will take to conduct a satisfactory appraisal interview. Far better to leave the time element open-ended and go on just so long as the interaction seems to be productive. In any event, ample time must be allowed for the manager to discuss to his complete satisfaction any points about the appraisal on which he has questions. In a lesser way, the same is true for the superior; he is intensely interested in the reaction of the manager to the results they have been discussing. So it is important that both parties have all the time they need to complete the process.

One point will take a little special handling on the part of the superior. Logically, this would seem to be the ideal time to do developmental planning for the next appraisal period. This is not true for several reasons. Both the superior and the subordinate are too close to the analytical process in which they have been involved. Both need a respite to be sure they have gained a proper perspective before attempting to apply remedies or set up a series of isometric exercises. What is more, as a rule neither is really expert in this part of the developmental field, and in most cases they should turn to the professional for help here.

Effectively, the boss and the manager have, with the conclusion of the interview, finished their personal contribution to this cycle of the developmental process. Of course, it is obvious that everything that has gone before is useless and an actual waste of time unless some action follows. Nothing is more sterile than for an organization to take this sort of look at a manager's performance and then neglect the follow-up which will be therapeutic and corrective of the weaknesses exposed. In the older efforts at management development, where so many subjective items were included, it was at the interview that the system broke down in a large percentage of the cases. Both superior and subordinate shied away from a situation so artificial and full of threat to both. Where objective goals are used, on the other hand, this element is lacking and both may proceed without emotional involvement along a course highly beneficial to the manager.

Developmental planning. Each of the other segments of this process has pointed to the planning necessary after the appraisal has been made. As noted, at this point both men would be wise to call on the services of the management development specialist. His training and everyday work make him especially able to see what particular learning experiences, new job assignments, or outside activities will be most likely to have a salutary effect on the development of our manager. This is certainly not to say that he should be a dictator of developmental experience. Rather, there should be a three-way interaction between the superior, the manager, and the specialist, with the specialist's advice receiving a little heavier weighting than that of the other two.

The important thing to remember is that the developmental planning for any appraisal period should *never* be considered as a discrete entity. It should always be related to the developmental process already under way and integrated with long-term planning looking well into the manager's future. One of the most delicate points of judgment in doing this planning is to determine the time that is exactly right for a given experience. For example, an MBA who has just entered management and is engrossed in his orientation into supervision is not at the point where job rotation should be forced into his developmental cycle. He needs so much of his concentration on the actual mechanics of supervision that it would be a mistake to put him into an unfamiliar function at this time. It is for this reason that job rotation is quite often delayed until the manager is well into middle management and is thoroughly expert in the practice of general management.

The specialist in his advisory capacity should also give attention to a proper mix of kinds of developmental activity. There should be some formal classroom work as the most economical way in which to teach theory, but this should be watched carefully so that it does not get a disproportionate amount of the effort. It is all too easy to fall into the habit of looking for a convenient course as the answer to every developmental problem.

Special assignments within the framework of the manager's own job can be very productive if the superior gives a real problem and closely follows the work done on it. This kind of project ordinarily demands quite tight control, as well as almost daily coaching from the supervisor. When properly chosen, a special assignment can be especially rewarding because of the quick and deep involvement of the manager in a problem which is near to him personally. He can also see a real personal gain from the solution of such problems within his own area of responsibility.

The three interested people should keep track of the chronology of outside seminars attended by the manager. The change of scene and new mix of interpersonal reactions will be very valuable when properly timed. This is comparable to the injection of new people into the organization in its effort of cross-pollenization of ideas.

Once again, time is of the essence in developmental planning. To avoid disruption and discontinuity of effort, there should never be more than a week or ten days' lapse between the interview and the adoption of the new plan for the coming appraisal period. The responsibility for the necessary coordination should be accepted and shared equally by the three parties concerned.

There is a further responsibility in the matter of developmental planning which should be shared by the superior and the specialist. The superior will be anxious that all the developmental planning for his part of the organization be integrated and interrelated. In the same way, the management development specialist looks to the desirability of integrating the developmental planning for the entire organization. He will never lose sight of the need for well-rounded development of all managers as they constitute the entire managerial hierarchy. In this sense, the hierarchy is exactly like an individual—unequal or lopsided developmental activity will make its operation inefficient just as it does in the case of an individual. A centralized overview of all developmental planning for the organization will make it much easier to be economical in budgeting the corporation's developmental hard dollars. These costs are always suspect, and the better they can be defended by management in general and by the management development specialist in particular, the easier it will be to maintain proper momentum in funding necessary developmental activity.

It is understandable why the first time or two through this appraisal cycle is a difficult experience for any manager. But there is one incontrovertible result of an honest effort to make it work: By the third or fourth time through the process, the manager will find it flowing smoothly, with his own apparent efforts minimized and with incontestable good effects showing up in his operation. His whole organization will be the better for it.

The management inventory. Good management demands that an accounting be kept of human resources in a company, as well as physical assets and money. Yet it is a strange fact that many modern businesses do not actually know the extent (in either kind or degree) of the skills, training, and experience of all their management personnel. The waste of time, effort, and money by these enterprises in trying to locate a particular skill is beyond belief. It is not uncommon for a company to advertise in *The Wall Street Journal,* send recruiters from coast to coast, and employ management search concerns, only to learn later to its considerable embarrassment that a member of its own management already possessed the skills it sought.

When this sort of slipshod procedure is followed, the damage to morale of present employees is quickly reflected in abnormally high attrition rates. Good people will not remain in an organization that shows this kind of carelessness with respect to its employees.

The raw data necessary for the establishment and maintenance of a functional management inventory is present in the bookkeeping done for the developmental appraisal system. With present electronic data processing machinery, the accumulation and recording of this information is not a formidable task. Essentially, there are only a few categories of data which are germane to the filling of new managerial positions, though there may at times be some concern about which items are necessary for entry in each of the categories.

Personal data. Some imagination must be shown in selecting items of a personal nature for storage in the management inventory data bank. It is the odd bits of information about a man which sometimes are the determinant of his getting the job. One man was picked as a chemistry teacher in his first teaching position because he could sing tenor. The school superintendent was determined to have a faculty male quartet for the coming school year. Chemistry teachers he could find on any bush; passable tenors were another matter entirely. Management development staff people will come to cultivate a sensitivity about personal data which will help them to select those items in the background of a manager which may later be significant when he is being looked at for a new job. Routinely, such items as age, national origin, height, weight, distinguishing personal characteristics, religion, marital status, and ages of assorted children are of direct interest. A recent trend in industry to become much more curious about a man's family is now being reflected in some of the data being recorded under this category. Because of greater interests in a manager's impact on his social ecology, this trend will probably persist and even increase.

Education. Today and in the future, the matter of education can only increase in importance in deciding the place any manager occupies in his company's management inventory. More should be recorded than the achievement of a specified degree from a specific school. Areas of concentration of study, individual subjects taken, and grades earned should all be included. Special note should be made of thesis or dissertation topics. Activities and special honors achieved are of significance, as is notation of the percentage of college expenses earned. This attention to detail should be intensified in looking at any graduate work done by the manager in question.

Training. A meticulous record must be kept of all training the manager receives, whether it is given on paid time or off-hours under company sponsorship or is obtained independently by the manager under his own steam. Of particular importance to the total picture is the chronology of this training, as well as its recency in some of the more exotic fields. It is often impossible to determine whether a particular bit of training was voluntary or imposed by supervision, but for our purposes the overall effect is the same. Many executives use a manager's training record as one of the critical items in separating candidates for final choice in a new and important job.

Work experience. The best single measure of a manager's progress and future potential is to chart out his work experience. Included should be kind, level, duration, and physical location of every job held by the manager. Within the company, it is also germane to record the name of the supervisor in each job held. This record will give a quick picture of breadth and depth of experience which will be invaluable in assessing a particular man's qualifications for a given position. Although it is not feasible to store in the memory bank performance appraisals for each position held, it is of the utmost importance that they be readily available from some other source.

Salary history. This item is perhaps the most sensitive of any which will go into the management inventory. Some companies prefer to keep these records entirely separate and insure access only to those with a proven need to know. Others do store this information in the memory bank but make entries in code, leaving the keys to this code in the hands of only a few individuals who carry total accountability for its divulgence. Like the experience record itself, this salary history is an excellent barometer of a man's progress and potential.

Secondary skills. It is sometimes difficult to elicit from either the man or his record lesser skills he possesses which, in connection with his primary field of work, would make just exactly the combination necessary for a fine promotion. The management development staff people in charge of the management inventory may have to do some probing on their own to follow up clues which they find in a man's record. For example, it is a fairly safe prediction that any man doing engineering or technical work would be sophisticated in some of the higher branches of mathematics. Or a manager who had had a liberal arts education would in all probability have had some work in one or more foreign languages. In these days, with such a wildly improbable proliferation of new technologies, it is never possible to predict when any given skill will suddenly have a premium attached to it.

Hobbies and leisure activities. It may seem odd to attach any importance to those activities which occupy a man in his leisure time. But to the trained observer they may be illuminating and add detail which will help to complete an overall picture of the manager. A man whose major hobbies are all concerned with outdoor physical activity would get the nod for assignment in some of the more rugged foreign countries over a man whose private life was sedentary or was concerned with intellectual pastimes. There is a constriction imposed by similar working conditions which makes it difficult to draw some of the fine discriminations necessary when picking a man for a particularly delicate assignment. This variable may be just the one to enable management to make the right choice.

If consistency is used in selection and in recording of details, the method of storage is not too critical. Many companies will find it convenient to keep their management inventory records on McBee cards, and the methods used extend all the way to the most exotic of computerization. What is of the highest importance is an objective use of the management inventory in making the best possible selection of personnel for promotion and new assignment. In larger companies, it is quite possible for a good man to be lost in a remote function and go for years without being considered for many jobs for which he has all the prime specifications. The losses to the company in attrition, unnecessary importation of outsiders, and lowered morale are not directly measurable. From the standpoint of economy alone, it is indefensible not to have exhausted in-house assets before going to the expense of bringing in new hires.

There should be no necessity to dwell on the importance of a centralized control and operation of the management inventory. It is absolutely fundamental that consistency of input and usage be continuous if proper results are to be had from this important management tool. Logically, the agent should be the management development staff people. Their intimate knowledge of all management personnel, their constant exposure to development and implementation of company policy, and their broad perspective of all functions make them the most natural administrator.

The key to the successful use of a management inventory is its maintenance on a day-to-day basis. A lapse of only a few weeks in the accumulation of data may be fatal in the selection of a key executive. Another factor which cannot be ignored is the staff position of management development specialists. They have no ax to grind; their involvement is with the total good for the entire company.

PERSONNEL RESEARCH

The application of statistical method and interpretation in the personnel field is of quite recent origin. It used to be that personnel directors worked by intuitive process and well-tended channels of communication when they needed information about the workforce. It must be admitted that in some cases their results came amazingly close to the truth. However, since the advent of the behavioral scientist on the industrial scene, information in amounts heretofore undreamed of is now available. The behavioral scientist, by careful design of an instrument and proper random sampling, can consistently get much more reliable information from a workforce than was ever done under the old process.

Morale surveys. Management continues to display a keen interest in the state of its employees' morale. Since the positive correlation between morale and such items as productivity, safety, cost control, and quality has been well established, it is of major importance to get a current reading on the spirit of an organization. The management development specialist, if he has had good training in industrial psychology, is able to put together a questionnaire which will be sufficiently neutral in statement as not to show any bias; at the same time, he can build internal checks on the honesty of the answers. The major point of difficulty in any morale survey is to convince the respondents that their answers will be treated anonymously, with no chance of the authorship being discovered by management. Of course, even more important than measuring morale itself is the discovery of the causes of any depression in the workforce. It is often possible to incorporate questions which will elicit responses indicative of the causes of employee dissatisfaction. For the most part, the average employee is glad to have an opportunity to express his dissatisfaction without fear of reprisal from his superiors. Although in some cases a morale survey may serve only to confirm suspected causes of unhappiness, in other cases entirely new causative factors may emerge, thus allowing for quick amelioration of the situation.

Course and program evaluation. During the early history of formal developmental activity, any attempted evaluation of a course or a program was purely subjective. It consisted usually of a two- or three-question form which probed the *feelings* of the trainees immediately after their exposure to the activity. Such emotion-packed responses are assuredly of questionable value. By use of proper instruments and careful and controlled follow-up, the behavioral scientist is able to determine much more specifically whether any permanent change has been effected by the course or program.

Another big contribution can be made to formal courses by having the behavioral scientist take charge of test validation. Item analysis and the accumulation and examination of test data can quickly result in testing instruments which are adequately valid and reliable. The behavioral scientist can make a significant contribution to the pedagogy of a management training organization without ever entering the classroom or the seminar.

"Tracking" the manager through his career. It has already been said in passing that management development staff should be given responsibility for the record keeping of the developmental process. In a more particular and definitive way, it should be one of the management development staff duties to plot the individual ca-

reer of every manager within the organization. In order that valid comparisons can be made between managers, it is essential that uniform methods be employed for charting progress and recording the development of individual managers. The matter logically belongs to a staff group whose accountability is companywide; this will minimize personal bias and prejudice.

The techniques and activities of personnel research are increasing rapidly in both scope and complexity. Properly conducted and properly evaluated, personnel research gives us a tool whose greatest effectiveness is in the *prevention* of situations which will result in personnel problems or discord. A notable leader in this part of management development has been Texas Instruments Incorporated. It has had more written about it and has come to exert more influence on industry at large in this area than any other single business entity. The Scott Myers article in particular * has had a tremendous influence on the thinking of American management since its publication, especially in those companies which have a heavy orientation toward engineering or technical employees.

Directly as a result of personnel research there is a concomitant which usually is also picked up by the management development specialist—the development of courses and programs to satisfy demonstrated needs. It is nearly impossible to separate these two activities, nor is it desirable to do so. By maintaining continuity of both overview and the creative process, a much better product will be the result. This is not to say, of course, that the comments and thinking of the line people should be ignored. They, after all, are the customers, and they will have to be satisfied if desired results are to be obtained.

* M. Scott Myers, "Who Are Your Motivated Workers?" *Harvard Business Review,* January–February 1964, pp. 73–88.

MANAGEMENT TRAINING

In many places in these pages reference has been made to various kinds of management training. Now let us consider it here purely as methodology. At the very outset, we should note two opposing philosophies concerning the management development staff's relationship and responsibility to the administration of management training. There can be no question that the staff members should be heavily involved in the development of course material and program content. But does it then follow that they should do the actual presentation, or the teaching of courses, on a routine and ongoing basis? Two things can happen when a management development staff becomes too deeply engrossed with teaching and the administration of programs. One is that the members' time becomes so curtailed that they will not be able to devote proper attention to their consultative activity, organizational planning, and executive development work. The second danger is that, if they give the image of a "training" group to the rest of the corporation, they will find it difficult to achieve the status with other managers that will insure acceptance in the consultative role.

Ordinarily, company managements will polarize strongly over this concept. Some will insist that their management development staffs be completely responsible for management training, even if this means they devote their entire time to it. Others perhaps will go to the opposite extreme and say their specialists will never engage in teaching except on a pilot basis as a program or course is first launched. If the latter viewpoint prevails, there is still a residual duty which the management development people must accept—they must be *responsible for* the recruiting and training of the people who will be the instructors. This in itself will produce some fine developmental activity for the line managers who are recruited as teachers. Instructing is one of the best of developmental experiences. Teaching exposes a person to a situation unique in his business career. Never before has he been forced to employ as much empathy or to make use of the last ounce of his sensitivity. This will happen to him when he enters the classroom as a teacher. It is an odd fact that managers in the classroom are more critical of their teachers than they are of other managers on the day-to-day job. They will challenge statements and philosophies expressed by their instructor which would be passed without comment if stated by a manager in his usual surroundings.

Management development staff can provide great strength to a management training course by carefully seeking out the manager who will be exactly right as an instructor, as well as providing a new and different method for the development of the instructor. Once the instructor is recruited, the staff people still have the duty of giving him pedagogical training if he has never taught before and of following and counseling on his progress in the classroom. Once designated and recruited as an instructor, the manager must have a successful experience in his teaching or the net result will be so negative as to cause him serious trouble.

Another decision should be made by the management development staff. That is whether a particular bit of management training should be done by in-house instructors, by a consultant team that is called in, or by an outside agency to which the trainees are sent. The basic circumstances surrounding the kind of training needed will be a governing factor here. If the training is concerned with some area totally connected with and peculiar to the company's operation, it should be done by company people. If, on the other hand, the area of involvement is in a technique or management practice new to the company, it will be more salutary to call on the services of a consultant who is expert in this particular field. Or, again, if the area of training has implications of involvement with other companies, the likelihood is that it will be far better to send the trainees to an outside seminar or to a university, where they will have the advantage of exposure to viewpoints and opinions of managers from other companies.

There is yet another responsibility with relation to management training that the staff specialist can never forget. He is charged with getting the best possible mileage from the training dollar. This is true whether we are speaking of hard dollars (actual cash spent for instruction or tuition) or the wooden dollars involved in spending the time of managers in training conducted during working hours. This responsibility includes attention to such details as size of class, length of training session, freedom from outside interruption, decent facilities, and a knowledge of the average span of attention of a given class. It is also necessary to make some fine discriminations as to the amount of training which will be effective during a given time. If the manager becomes involved in so many training efforts that he finds it difficult to do his regular job, there can be only one choice: Some of the training must be postponed for a better time.

One final charge must be left on the shoulders of the staff specialist. He is in the best position to determine when a good balance of training activity has been achieved by a given manager. As the keeper of development records, the staff man can best ascertain when a pragmatic mix has been arrived at for the various managers in the organization. He alone is in the best position to blow the whistle when he sees evidence of training being done for training's sake. There can be no greater crime against the concept of managerial development.

SPECIAL MANAGERIAL EXPERIENCES

A major part of any man's management training will consist of special assignments tailored for him personally. The man's supervisor will ordinarily be the instigator of this kind of developmental activity, but quite often the services of the management development specialist will be solicited to be sure that the experience will be so designed as to be most functional for the manager concerned.

It may be that the performance appraisal has resulted in identifying a need for more development of the manager's planning function. The superior might then give him responsibility for developing the unit's goals for the forthcoming six months or a year. It would be understood that the manager would come back to his supervisor with a complete package, which he had developed alone, and that the two of them would then reconcile their ideas to the satisfaction of the superior before formal adoption of the goals for the organization. A move often made with the intent of developing younger men who are showing promise is to give them broadening experience as "loaned executives" for Good Neighbor drives or as advisers to Junior Achievement clubs. The rationale for this type of assignment is that broader experience can be had quickly, in an area where there will be small risk for the company.

The manager at the threshold of the executive level, for whom the desire is to increase his conceptualization powers, may be assigned to professional organizations for the industry, where his interactions will give him exposure to the thinking of men from many other enterprises. Throughout all this kind of activity, the management development staff should maintain, at the minimum, a record keeping and coordinating hand at the helm.

Job rotation has already been mentioned in another context as a developmental activity. Suffice it to say here that if it is properly done it can be one of the better devices for bringing a man along. This is the easier way for a manager to increase his company knowledge in both scope and depth, while at the same time giving him insight into the problems of managers in other functions. This activity can be the catalyst by which a specialist is transformed into a generalist, which must be done before he can function effectively as an executive.

There is a developing trend for the use of special study teams to perform internal audits on a particular function of an enterprise. At a manager's request, a team is formed to come in and make an intensive study of his organization. This usually takes 60 to 90 days. The whole purpose, of course, is to look for methods of streamlining and tightening up the group so that it will function more economically. The experience gained from membership in one of these study teams is hard to duplicate elsewhere. The work is demanding, difficult, and extremely objective. Members of the team are required to be as completely objective as they find it possible; there can be no place for sentimentality or weakness. Once or twice through this process may be the most effective developmental assignment the manager will ever have.

Because of the direction our country is taking in increasingly complex technologies, it may be felt necessary to send a manager back to formal school for new technical information, even until he is well into middle management. The granting of paid leaves of absence to return for an advanced degree is becoming commonplace in American industry. The time and money spent will constitute an investment, rather than an expense. Even if an actual degree is not the objective, many managers high in the hierarchy may derive a great deal of good from an academic year spent on a Sloan Fellowship at such schools as Harvard, M.I.T., or Stanford. Many other advanced management programs are used by companies in the development of their executives and key managers.

The fully rounded development of any manager demands that he have time in both line and staff managership. Empathy must be there for the posts themselves and for the thinking of both types of posts before an integrated operation can be achieved which will get the best results for the entire enterprise.

The special assignment part of the manager's development is what makes his training unique and takes into account his individual needs as distinct from those of any other person. More and more time and care will be demanded in the choice of these activities as the manager matures. He himself, his superior, and the development staff must work as a team in laying out the best possible road for his growth. His effectiveness and usefulness to the company can be magnified many times with proper attention to this area.

CONSULTATION IN THE MANAGEMENT DEVELOPMENT SPECIALIST'S JOB

The consultative function in the management development staff man's job is on the increase. If he is to better his efficiency and exert greater influence, this trend must continue. In delineating the consultative part of the management development job, it is necessary to define some terms. It should be noted that the definitions given here are purely operational.

Development. This may be understood as a gradual change through a combination of forces or methods. (It is also assumed that the valences of these vectors will always be positive.)

Consultation. As used here this is acting as a sounding board, then giving help in appraising a situation—including the identification of sound alternative actions—and providing specialized knowledge and information.

Management development consultation. This is defined here as help in appraising organizational or individual management capabilities and needs and in identifying goals as well as methods of improving them.

Management development a line function. The person-to-person work in the development of managers is a line function and should continue to be so. The staff role in management development is to identify a management development discipline, supply direction, show benefits, generate top management's interest to perpetuate sustained action in the proposed program, provide relevant consultation, and render specialized services or coordination.

Distinction between consultation and counseling. In taking a professional approach to the management development function, the staff will welcome, even solicit, consultative work. When properly done, this can be the most creative and influential contribution of the management development specialist to the welfare of the organization.

There must be an understanding by the consultant of some of the related distinctions or precautions he must observe. For example, where systems are involved, he should go no further than problem identification. He should never attempt to solve operational problems. He must never allow the line manager to abdicate.

Personal counseling, on the contrary, will be avoided whenever possible by management development staff members. The dangers inherent to the long-range relationships are too obvious to need emphasis here. If the situation arises wherein the client insists on baring his problem to the specialist, the latter should act as a referral agent and then make a graceful exit.

The climate. True management development is both an attitude and a way of life. Before the specialist can make a significant contribution to the development of management personnel, he must observe some unalterable prerequisites. There are "foundation" abilities and knowledge. Some of these are innate; some are acquired; all of them may be increased with education or relevant experience.

- There must be comprehension of the client's business environment, significant objectives, policies, and operating constraints.
- There must be a strong grasp of management principles and methodology, along with their applicacation in varying kinds of situations. Concomitant with this must be a real sensitivity to the proper timing of a proposed change.
- Of fundamental importance is an understanding of appraisal, selection, and development of individual managers. This must go far beyond a superficial view of appraisal. The specialist must have a knowledge of program possibilities and, above all, how best to avoid "course" traps.
- There must be an ability to relate all of the foregoing in the analysis of significant organizational capabilities or problems.

- The specialist must have personal "presence" and communicative skill.
- Of extreme importance, the specialist must have the perception and courage to concern himself with matters of innovation and significance.
- There must be expertise in problem analysis. The consultant must relate to the organizational goals and be able to apply special techniques, such as the functional audit, while at all times keeping these in *management development* context.
- The consultant must be expert in conference leadership and the technique of Socratic dialogue.
- The specialist must maintain a critical evaluation of new techniques and disciplines, and he must be prepared to adopt and integrate into his operations those which appear promising.

Top management must continue to give active support. The implementation of top management's support must be by communication to line management. No staff man will ever convince the line men of the ego-involvement of their superiors. The final test must be that line managers will be held *accountable* for the development of their people.

The consultative function. After these prerequisites have been satisfied, we should now be ready to devote our best efforts to the implementation of this aspect of our functional duties. However, here again, a definitive line of involvement must be followed.

- The first step in getting this relationship with the line is to insure that management development personnel will not be seen as an operating clique. Fraternization of the "management development types" at lunch and in the business scene should

be minimized to provide more time for interaction with clients.

- The way to start is to do something useful. Currently, the best points of entry are the replacement tables, executive nominees, and the Advanced Management Program (AMP); then it is possible to capitalize strongly in this entry.
- The management development staff must be content to remain in the background. Line management will get the credit. *Management development is a line function.*
- Completed staff work is essential. Nothing can be more damaging to the whole charisma than one piece of incomplete or sloppy work.
- By increasing competency in the use of the tools at his command and by performing worthwhile service in his consultative capacity, the management development man will come to have a real, beneficial influence on the management of the company.

Contacts and levels of consultative action. It must be remembered that in a cost-conscious organization, the management development function will always be undermanned and running lean. For efficiency, most of management development's consultative action in the foreseeable future will be at the executive level or in the middle-management area. The specialist cannot justify indiscriminate response to requests of first-line management for consultative activity.

IO

Summary

THE central theme which has been reiterated throughout this volume is two-pronged: First, the developmental process which any manager undergoes is the product of his own activity; second, it must be considered and thought of as a continuous function. If we try to break down managerial development into a series of discrete components, the perspective will be lost and the resultant product will be an inferior one. The third thesis on which this discussion has rested is that management development is a line function and that the very necessary work done by the management development specialist is purely staff, usually of a consultative nature.

One of the larger problems in American industry today is to lure the average manager into accepting his responsibilities for his own development and that of others. There is danger in the situation where the manager pays lip service to the idea of manager development, but feels he has completed his entire duty in this direction if he has identified and taken a course or two. Course work as such is a very inefficient change agent of human behavior. The elements necessary for change to take place are identification, involvement, and activity. If the process of development, whatever it may be, is openly adopted by the manager, if it is enough a product of his own analytical thinking for him to feel ownership of it, and if a real response has occurred, there will be a change in behavior. Thereafter, the continuation of this change follows the established laws for habit formation.

Whatever attitude is maintained by top management of an enterprise toward management development can be nothing but the simple reflection of the company's philosophy. This is why it is imperative that the philosophy be verbalized and recorded, so that management in general can feel secure in establishing its developmental practices.

Continued stress must be placed by all managers, individually and as a team, on the matter of uniformity of development. A symmetrical configuration is essential for smooth and efficient usage of the available manpower. It is at this point that the management development specialist will do his work as a catalyst. It is his job to reconcile and join individual efforts at manager development into a unified whole. The unique contribution of management development staff is in *organizational* development.

Because results of developmental activity can never be accurately quantified, resistance is common in management circles to the outlay of hard dollars for this purpose. More than one company has found it expedient to budget a small percentage of either revenue or undivided profits for management development on a continuing basis. This assumes that philosophically the matter of development of personnel is considered as an investment, with no immediate return on a dollars-and-cents computation. This has its parallel in the money spent by some of the larger companies for pure research. They know that probability will eventually return a profit on the amount invested.

This whole conceptualization of management development is based on complete acceptance of the idea of management by results. No progress can be forecast unless realistic goals and objectives are established by each manager in the area of his responsibility. Moreover, implicit in this is the eventual involvement of all employees, so that they will make a willing contribution toward the achievement of the set goals because of their ego-involvement.

Top management must remember that, in a medium-size or large organization, there will be a normal bell curve in the distribution of both rates and extent of the development of managers. Never will it be possible to expect anything like uniformity in the rate of growth. Another item which provides frustration for the organization watchers is the significant number of "promising" young managers who, for one reason or another, never fulfill the potential ascribed to them. Just as maddening are the cases of managers who follow a normal or even good developmental pattern, then suddenly peak out and fail to show any further growth. These happenings are statistically perfectly normal in a population of managers, and allowance must be made for their occurrence in working with executive nominee groups and replacement tables. The important thing here is to make the best assessment possible for each event and be prepared to make the necessary structural alterations in the organization to strengthen the weak spots.

Considerable emphasis (but certainly not too much)

has been placed on the need to have the managerial group in any enterprise flexible enough to adjust for the many changes which will come to every industry and in increasing numbers over the coming years. The management of change is already one of the most important aspects of any manager's work, and it will continue to be so. It presents a very particular challenge to plan for the training and development of managers in aspects of their job which do not even exist today.

The unique genius of American business and industry has been the foundation for the greatness achieved by our country. If we as a nation retain our pre-eminent position, it will be because our industrial population continues to outproduce, at a ponderable cost, the rest of the world. This can happen only if our managerial people also continue to lead, innovate, and outstrip our competition. Whether they succeed will depend upon the state of health of our management development in the future.

Index

achievement, measurement of, 200–205

aerospace industry, 23

aging executive, effect of on organization, 185–187; *see also* executive; retired executive

American Management Association, 164–165; decision-making seminars of, 83; impact of on management development, 13

appraisal process: achievement measurement and, 200–205; development planning and, 205–208; goal setting and, 197–200; interview in, 202–205; in management development, 192–213; management inventory in, 208–209; personal data in, 209; special assignments and, 219–221

appraisal standards, in presupervisory selection, 47–49

apprenticeship, managerial, 26; *see also* presupervisory selection

"assistant" role, 89

autonomy, in new supervisor, 94

Baruch, Bernard M., 179

Bass, B. M., 120

behavioral scientist, emergence of, 15–16

"best-machinist" method of selection, 32–33

Blake, Robert, 84–85, 88–91

board of directors: executive's contacts with, 164; in executive selection, 145

Cabell, James Branch, 90

candidate(s): flow of, 41; interviewing of, 38; management commitment to, 71–72; number of, 42–45; for presupervisory training, 50–72 (*see also* presupervisory training); promotion of, 44; self-development of, 41; "tailored training package" for, 70; training needs of, 49–50; volunteering of, 40

chain of command, new supervisor in, 77–78

change, planning and, 23

classroom methods, in presupervisory training, 60–62

college graduates, management potential in, 131

college recruitment, supervisory selection and, 43

communication: fetish of, 14; by manager, 29; with middle manager, 129; in presupervisory training, 61–62; project concept and, 23

company philosophy: manager and, 17; mandatory retirement in, 188–189; and presupervisory selection, 34–37; *see also* company policy company policy: disagreement with, 35–36; executive and, 151; and presupervisory selection, 34–37

computer: in decision making, 82–83; manager selection and, 135

conceptual skills: in executive, 150–151, 162; in first-line supervisor, 74; as selective criteria, 45; *see also* technical skills

conference leadership, as fad, 14

conservatism, in middle manager, 104–105

consultant, retired executive as, 179

consultant-specialists, staff of, 11

consultation, vs. counseling, 222

consultative function, in management development, 221–225

control, line functions and, 24

cooperation, vs. competition, 78

coordination, managerial, 25

cost, managerial styles and, 92–95

counseling, vs. consultation, 222

"country club" manager, 85, 90

creativity, retirement and, 188

deaths, new management and, 31, 131

decentralized organization, dangers in, 35–36

decision making: in executive, 163; management slowness in, 81–84; managerial, 26–27; mathematical models in, 135; middle management and, 103; and retiring executive, 180; simulation models in, 82–83; training in, 81

Defense Department, U.S., 134–135

delegation: in appraisal process, 194–195; failure in, 162

development: for executive, 161–166; of senior executive, 155–158; *see also* management development

development staff or specialists: consultative function of, 221–225; executive potential and, 135–136; function of, 137; generalists and, 160; importance of, 158; knowledge required in, 146; management training and, 217–218; and retiring executive, 175–176; selection committee and, 39; senior executive and, 156–157; supervisory training and, 97; *see also* executive development; management development

education, in appraisal process, 209

EIMP (early identification of management personnel), 46

emotional stability, in retiring executive, 175–177

employee morale, 212–214

executive: aging, *see* aging executive; architectural competence in, 165–166; "challenge" for, 166–167; conceptual skills in, 150–151, 154, 159, 162; contacts with other company executives, 164; creativity of, 188; decision making by, 163; decreased income at retirement, 173; development of, 155–158; development time for, 161–163; distinguishing qualities or characteristics, 147–150; emptiness facing at retirement, 173; fear or panic in, 163; feedback from, 168; as generalist, 158–161; interpersonal relationships of, 170; isolation of, 153–155; job enrichment for, 164–165; leadership in, 164–165, 171; long-range planning of, 153–154, 178; "look-alike" successor for, 184; loss of prestige at retirement, 172–173; vs. middle manager, 150–152; motivation in, 166; on-the-job training for, 163; organization structure and, 171; phasing out at retirement, 169–190; physical health of, 188; policy-making authority of, 149; preparing for retirement, 175–176; productivity of, 169–170; profitability of, 170; public relations and, 151–152; quality of contribution, 170; replacement for, 177–185; responsibility of, 148–149; salary or compensation for, 148; security needs of, 182; status of, 149–150; training and development for, 161–166; training of replacement for, 177–180; university courses for, 164, 221; weaknesses in, 157; wrong person as replacement for, 183

executive development, 147–168; research courses in, 164; *see also* development; management development

executive potential: conventional methods in recognizing, 131–144

executive replacement, techniques in, 145–146, 169–190

"executive search" consultants, 143

executive selection: methodology in, 145–146, 191–225; from outside company, 142–144; performance review in, 139–140; salary history in, 140, 210–211; span of control in, 144

executive training, *see* training

fads: American business and, 13, 16; in managerial styles, 87; projective tests as, 46

family relationships, of new supervisor, 79

favoritism: in new supervisor, 37, 77; in presupervisory selection, 32

fear, in executive, 163

Federal Aviation Authority, 135

feedback: in middle management, 119–121; in presupervisory training, 61

first-line supervisor: care in selection of, 34–35; conceptual skills of, 74; decision making by, 81–84; development staff and, 157; as maker of product, 37; responsibilities of, 101; technical skills of, 73–74; *see also* supervisor

foreman, temporary, 57–60

gamesmanship, in middle management, 107

generalist: need for, 158–159; vs. specialist, 158–161

goals, quantifiable, 198

goal setting, in management appraisal setting, 197–200

Great Books program, 159

Great Britain, management development in, 12

grid concept, in managerial styles, 84–86

group cohesiveness, 92

group dynamics, in presupervisory training, 66–67

halo effect, middle manager and, 121–124

Harvard case method, 65

Harvard University, 164, 221

Hawthorne experiments, 13, 16

hero worship, middle manager and, 122
hobbies and leisure activities, 211–213
homework, of new supervisor, 79
human relations, experiments in, 13, 16

industrial psychologist, 16
intelligence, quality of, 28–29
internal audit teams, 220
interview, appraisal, 202–205
isolation: of executive, 153–155; of middle manager, 111

Japan, management development in, 12
Jennings, E. M., 45 n.
job enrichment, for executive, 166
job rotation: appraisal process and, 206, 220; for middle managers, 125–126
job training, for new supervisor, 95; *see also* training

Katz, Robert, 21, 73

"lab group," as recent fad, 15
labor relations, middle manager and, 114–115
leadership: aging executive and, 186; in executive, 165; as fad, 14; of middle manager, 120; by new supervisor, 93; in pre-supervisory training, 61; "trait-ist" theory of, 28
Leadership Psychology and Organizational Behavior (Bass), 120 n.
leaves of absence, 220–221
liaison, managerial, 24–25
line functions, major, 22–24
line management: new supervisor in, 86–87; selection committee and, 39

"loaned executives," 219
loyalty, 29

management: "candidates" for, 31–34; as line function, 18; middle, *see* middle management; "new blood" in, 31–32; participative, 94; projective tests and, 46; "psychology" of, 46
management action plan (MAP), 62–65
management consultants, executive search by, 143
management decision, affirming of by candidate, 68–69
management development:
achievement measurement in, 200–205; American Management Association and, 13; appraisal process in, 192–213; behavioral scientist in, 15–16; bell curve in, 228; climate of, 223–225; communication and, 14; consultation in, 221–225; as continuing process, 19; defined, 10–11; functional interrelationships in, 30; goal setting and, 197–200; historical development of, 12–13; line and staff responsibilities in, 18–19; as line function, 222, 225; management support of, 224; methodology of, 191–225; operations research and, 135–136; personnel research in, 213–215; place in organization, 11–12; senior executive and, 156; uniformity of, 227; *see also* development staff or specialists; executive development
management inventory, 208, 212–213
Management of Ineffective Performance, The (Minor), 187

management training, 216–219; *see also* presupervisory training; training

manager: achievement measurement in, 200–205; aging, 169 ff; appraisal of, 192–195; attributes and characteristics of, 28–29; bias in selection of, 132; "calling" of, 26; company philosophy and, 17; compromises by, 17; cyclical functions of, 25–26; decisions by, 26–27; education of, 209–210; as generalist, 159; goal setting by, 197–200; high-potential, 131–134; hobbies and leisure activities of, 211–213; human skills required of, 21; integrity of, 29; interview with boss, 202–205; job of, 21–30; liaison and coordination in, 24–25; major line functions, 22–24; motivation of, 28; neurotic, 29; performance appraisal of, 194–197; personal data on, 209; planning by, 22; "playing God" by, 48; pressures on, 106–107, 116–118; responsibility accepted by, 18, 226; responsibility to, 10; salary history, 140, 210–211; second selection process for, 130–146; secondary skills of, 211; self-development in, 29–30; sensitivity of, 29; special assignments for, 219–221; subordination to organization, 27; tough-mindedness of, 29; "tracking" of through career, 214–215; training record for, 210; type casting of, 131; underachieving, 201

manager selection: conventional methods in, 139–144; research and development in, 134–139; *see also* presupervisory selection

managerial ethics, 71–72

Managerial Grid, concept of, 84–86

managerial responsibility, concept of, 18, 226

managerial styles: changes in, 94–95; peer group influences in, 87; production and, 92–95; selection by supervisor, 84–92

MAP (management action plan), 62–65

Maslow, A. H., 22 n.

Massachusetts Institute of Technology, 14, 164, 221

MBA degree, 51, 100, 159, 206

McGregor, Douglas, 14, 84, 88, 91

methodology, of management development, 191–225; *see also* management development

middle management: as "desert," 102–129; meaning of term, 102–103; responsibility and pressures of, 106–107; seminars in, 124–125; *see also* middle manager

middle manager: coaching by supervisors, 126; communication with, 128–129; community relations activities of, 126; conservatism of, 104; decision-making authority of, 103–104; delegation by, 112, 162; development activities for, 128–129; development of by management, 127–129; employee dependency on, 122; vs. executive, 150–152; as expert, 110; feedback to, 119–120; goals of, 118; halo effect in, 121–124; high-potential, 131; isolation of, 111; job rotation for, 125–126; leadership of, 120; line relationships of, 117; management's responsibility for developing, 127–129; neglected status of, 105–111; organization and, 17; pressures on, 106–107, 116–118; self-development in, 109; self-image of, 119; sensitivity of, 116; spot check by, 119–120; strikes and, 114–115; as supervisory style, 91; supportive attitude for, 128; time and work pressures on, 116–118; training and development for, 124–126; voluntary job resignations and, 115–116

Mills College, 158

Minor, John B., 187

morale surveys, 213–214

Moses, leadership precepts by, 12

motivation, as manager, 28; *see also* goals

Mouton, Jane, 84–85, 88–91

Myers, M. Scott, 215

NASA (National Aeronautics and Space Administration), 135

National Training Laboratories, 15

nepotism, in presupervisory selection, 32

neuroticism, 29, 46

night work, 79

objectivity, of manager, 28

off-hour activities, of new supervisors, 99

one-man business, 12

operations research, 135

Oregon, University of, 187

organization: aging executive and, 185–187; change and, 23; decentralized, 35; individual manager and, 17; individual's career and, 100–101; management development in, 11–12; manager's subordination to, 27; "new blood" in, 181; and retirement of executive, 179–185; supervisor's concept of, 75

Organization Man, The (Whyte), 17, 45 n.

outside talent, recruitment of, 142–144

overpermissiveness, by supervisor, 93

participative management, 94

Pasteur, Louis, 137

peer evaluation: in executive selection, 141; in manager selection, 133; *see also* peer group

peer group: attitude changes in, 78; managerial style and, 87; in middle management, 107

performance appraisal, 139–140, 192–195; *see also* appraisal process

personal data, in appraisal process, 209

personnel research, 213–215

PERT (program evaluation and review technique), 135

Pigors incident process, 65

planning: in appraisal process, 205–208; change and, 23; developmental, 205–208; goal setting and, 198–199; as line function, 22; in presupervisory training, 69; supervisory candidates in, 44

policy statement, in presupervisory selection, 34–35

position description, in appraisal process, 194–197

premanagement training, 52–53; *see also* presupervisory training; training

pressures, in middle management, 106–107, 116–118

presupervisory selection, 31–50; appraisal standards in, 47–49; "best machinist" method in, 32–33; "boss" image in, 48–49; candidate volunteering in, 40–41; chance in, 42; college recruiting and, 43; company policy and, 34–37; conceptual and technical skills in, 44–45; first-line and second-line supervisors in, 34–35; interview in, 38; microtome technique in, 33–34; nepotism and favoritism in, 32; number of candidates in, 42–44; objectivity in, 47; propinquity in, 33; psychological testing in, 45–46; seniority in, 32; supervisory selection committees and, 37–40; training needs in, 49–50; volunteering and, 40; *see also* executive selection; manager; presupervisory training

presupervisory training, 9–10, 51–72; "best" method in, 69–70; classroom methods in, 60–62; extent and depth of, 52–54; feedback in, 61; group dynamics in, 66–67; "homework" in, 66; length of program in, 55; management decision in, 68–69; management ethics in, 71–72; management judgment in, 71–72; methods in, 54–67; objectives of, 53; outside reading in, 67; progress reports in, 56; role playing in, 66–67; seminar approach in, 65–67; tailored "package" in, 70; temporary foreman in, 57–60; total job in, 53

product, first-line supervisor and, 37

production, managerial style and, 92–95

product life, planning and, 22

project concept, 23

projective tests, 45–46

promotion, supervisory candidate and, 44

propinquity, in presupervisory selection, 33

protocol, for new supervisor, 77

psychological testing, 45–46

public relations, executive and, 151

Reddin, R. J., 84 n.

research and development, executive interest in, 167

research and program development, need for, 134–139

responsibility: of executive, 148–149; of first-line supervisor, 101; line and staff, 18–19; managerial, 18, 226

retired executive, 169 ff; as consultant, 179; efficiency of, 187; emotional syndrome of, 173–174; expertise of, 189–190; help for, 175–177; organizational dynamics and, 179–180; security needs of, 182; self-discipline in, 178; *see also* retirement

retirement: age at, 187–188; manager replacement at, 130; mandatory, 187–190; new management and, 31; transition to, 169–190

role playing, in presupervisory training, 66–67

salary, executive, 148

salary history: in appraisal process, 140, 195, 210–211

second-line supervisor, in trainee program, 57; *see also* supervisor

selection committees, in presupervisory selection, 37–40

self-analysis, in new supervisor, 86

self-confidence, 83

self-development, 98–100

seminars, for new supervisor, 65–67

senior executive: development of, 155–158; replacement for, 177–185; *see also* executive

seniority, promotion and, 32
sensitivity, of manager, 29
sensitivity training, 15
simulation models, in decision making, 82–83
Sloan Fellowships, 164, 221
social groups, changes in following promotion, 80
span of control, in executive selection, 144
special assignments, 219–221
specialist: appraisal process and, 206; making "generalist" of, 158–161
speech construction, for new supervisor, 99
staff, developmental, *see* development staff or specialists; line management staffing, planning and, 23
Stanford University, 164, 221
strikes, middle manager and, 114–115
subordinates: evaluation by, 141; motivation of, 22
superior-subordinate relationships, 18, 22, 68–69, 154; in appraisal process, 194–195, 204–205; changes in, 76–77; and coaching of middle management, 126; executive selection and, 141; hero image in, 122–123; managerial style and, 92–95; of middle manager, 112; retiring executive and, 176
supervisor: autonomy of, 94; certificates for, 100; changed interpersonal relationships of, 76–80; competition vs. cooperation of, 78; in decision-making process, 81–84; delegation by, 162; "efficiency model" in, 88–89; employee behavior and, 92; vs. executive, 151–152; extracurricular volunteering by, 75;

favoritism in, 77; first-line, *see* first-line supervisor; friends and enemies of, 78; as instructor, 63; isolation of, 113–114; leadership qualities of, 93; managerial styles and, 84–92; as "man in the middle," 90–91; off-hour courses for, 99; organization overview by, 75; organization success and, 100–101; overpermissive, 85, 90, 93; peer groups of, 76, 80; "pot of gold" style in, 91; self-analysis in, 86; self-confidence in, 83–84; self-development in, 98–100; "special assistant" role, 89; technical skills of, 44–45, 73–74; testing by crew members, 74; training of, 95–98; training vs. style in, 88; transition period in, 73–101; trial-and-error discovery in, 88; upward social mobility of, 80; volunteering by, 75; wife and family of, 79
supervisory candidate, *see* candidate
supervisory development, *see* supervisor; management development
supervisory trainee: concepts of, 55–57; as temporary foreman, 57–60; *see also* presupervisory training

technical skills: first-line supervisor and, 73–74; as selection criteria, 44–45
technology, expansion of, 11
testing, psychological, 45–46
Texas Instruments Incorporated, 215
textbooks, in presupervisory training, 67
T-groups, as fad, 15
thefts, of company property, 114

Theory X, Theory Y concepts, 84–85, 91
time, in developmental planning, 207; pressures of, 106–107, 116–118
Toastmasters organization, 98–99
trainee: confused status of, 58–59; program length for, 55–57; *see also* presupervisory training
trainer, training of, 137
training: in appraisal process, 210; course development in, 138; in decision making, 81; for executive, 161–163; of new supervisor, 95–98 (*see also* supervisor); objectives of, 53, 68–69; presupervisory, *see* presupervisory training; of trainer, 137

transition period, in becoming supervisor, 73–101

underachievement, 201
university courses, 164, 221

voluntary resignations, 115
volunteering, in supervisory selection, 40

wagon-and-star mechanism, in middle management, 121–124
Wall Street Journal, 85, 208
Wert, Robert, 158
Whyte, William H., 17, 45 n.
wildcat strikes, 114–115

About the Author

ELTON T. REEVES is supervisor of off-hours management training, consultant for the Materials Department of the Airplane Division, and editor of a bimonthly publication on management development for a large Western corporation. He was awarded his B.S. from the University of Idaho and his M.A. from the University of Washington, and he has done graduate work in industrial psychology at Louisiana State University.

Mr. Reeves has been a high school instructor, high school principal, supervisory rubber chemist at U.S. Rubber Company, pharmaceutical detail man at Lederle Laboratories Division of American Cyanamid Company, industrial relations man for Kaiser Aluminum & Chemical Corporation, and corporate training director at Warwick Electronics, Inc. He was management development coordinator before assuming his present responsibilities.

Mr. Reeves is author of a number of published articles and a member of the American Society for Training and Development.